SACHIN YADAV

DIRECTOR OF BHOJPURI FILM

MR VIVEK KUMAR PANDEY

XpressPublishing
An imprint of Notion Press

XpressPublishing
An imprint of Notion Press

Old No. 38, New No. 6
McNichols Road, Chetpet
Chennai - 600 031

First Published by Notion Press 2020
Copyright © Mr Vivek Kumar Pandey 2020
All Rights Reserved.

ISBN 978-1-64805-431-0

Contents

• iii •

CHAPTER ONE

Sachin Yadav

"Bhojpuri" redirects here. For other uses, see Bhojpuri (disambiguation).

This article contains Indic text. Without proper rendering support, you may see question marks or boxes, misplaced vowels or missing conjuncts instead of Indic text.

Bhojpuri

भोजपुरी (Bhōjpurī) • ???????

The word "Bhojpuri" in Devanagari script

Native toIndia and Nepal

RegionPurvanchal-Bhojpur

EthnicityBhojpuri

Native speakers

51 million, partial count (2011 census)[1]

(additional speakers counted under Hindi)

Language family

Indo-EuropeanIndo-IranianIndo-AryanEastern Zone (Magadhan)Bihari languages

Bhojpuri

Dialects

Northern (Gorakhpuri, Sarawaria, Basti, Padrauna)

Western (Purbi, Benarsi)

Southern (Kharwari)

Nagpuria (Sadari)

Tharu Bhojpuri

Madheshi

Domra

Musahari

Caribbean Hindustani

· Trinidadian Hindustani

(Trinidadian Bhojpuri,

Plantation Hindustani,

Gaon ke Bolee)

· Guyanese Hindustani

(Aili Gaili)

· Sarnami Hindoestani

Fiji Hindi

Mauritian Bhojpuri

South African Bhojpuri (Naitali)[2]

Writing system

Kaithi

Devanagari[3]

Perso-Arabic (Moribund)
   Official status
   Official language in
    Fiji (as the Fiji Hindi dialect)
   Recognised minority
language in
    India (as a second language in Jharkhand)[4]
  Nepal (as a national regional language)
 Mauritius
   Language codes
   ISO 639-2bho
   ISO 639-3bho – inclusive code
Individual codes:
hns – Caribbean Hindustani
hif – Fiji Hindi
   Glottologbhoj1246[5]
   Linguasphere59-AAF-sa

This article contains IPA phonetic symbols. Without proper rendering support, you may see question marks, boxes, or other symbols instead of Unicode characters. For an introductory guide on IPA symbols, see Help:IPA.

Bhojpuri (/ˌboʊdʒˈpʊəri/;[6] भोजपुरी (help·info)) is an Indo-Aryan language spoken in northern-eastern India and the Terai region of Nepal.[3] It is chiefly spoken in western Bihar and eastern Uttar Pradesh.[6][7] Sociolinguistically, Bhojpuri is considered one of several Hindi dialects.[8] The language is an official language of Nepal[citation needed] and a minority language in Guyana, Trinidad and Tobago, Suriname, South Africa, and Mauritius.[9][10]

Fiji Hindi, an official language of Fiji, is a variant of Awadhi and Bhojpuri. Caribbean Hindustani, another variant of Awadhi and Bhojpuri, is spoken by the Indo-Caribbean people.[11] It has experienced lexical influence from Caribbean English in Trinidad and Tobago and in Guyana. In Suriname, languages that have lexically influenced it include Sranan Tongo Creole, Surinamese Dutch, and English. Another dialect is spoken in Mauritius; its use is declining, and As of 2000 it is spoken by about 5% of the country's population.[12]

Contents
1Geographic distribution
2Dialects
3Phonology
4Writing system
5Politeness
6Status
7Literature
8Media
9Common words
9.1Weekdays
9.2Common phrases
10Example text
11See also
12References
13External links
Geographic distribution[edit]
Bhojpuri-speaking region in India

The Bhojpuri-speaking region in India borders the Awadhi-speaking region to the west, the Nepali-speaking region to the north, the Magahi- and Maithili-speaking regions to the east, and the Magahi- and Bagheli-speaking regions to the south.[3] In Nepal, Bhojpuri is a major language.[10] Bhojpuri-speaking Muslims live in Bangladesh. Their population is lower than that of Bhojpuri speakers in Mauritius, South Africa, Fiji, and Caribbean nations.[citation needed][clarification needed]

Bhojpuri is spoken by descendants of indentured labourers brought in the 19th and early 20th centuries for work in plantations in British colonies. These Bhojpuri speakers live in Mauritius, Trinidad and Tobago, Guyana, Suriname, Fiji, Jamaica, South Africa, and other parts of the Caribbean.[9][10][13]

Dialects[edit]

Bhojpuri has several dialects: Southern Standard Bhojpuroi, Northern Standard Bhojpuri, Western Standard Bhojpuri[14], and Nagpuria Bhojpuri.[15][10] The first three are the major dialects.

Southern Standard Bhojpuri is prevalent in the Shahabad district (Buxar, Bhojpur, Rohtas, and Kaimur districts) and the Saran region (Saran, Siwan and Gopalganj districts) in Bihar, and the eastern Azamgarh (Ballia and Mau districts) and Varanasi (eastern part of Ghazipur district) regions in Uttar Pradesh. The dialect is also known as Kharwari. It can be further divided into Shahabadi, Chapariyah, and Pachhimahi.[16]

Northern Bhojpuri is common in the western Tirhut division (east and west Champaran districts) in Bihar, and Gorakhpur division (Deoria, Kushinagar, Gorakhpur, and Maharajganj districts) and Basti division (Basti, Sidharthanagar, and Sant Kabir Nagar districts) in Uttar Pradesh. It is also spoken in Nepal.[17]

Western Bhojpuri is prevalent in the areas of Varanasi (Varanasi, Chandauli, Jaunpur, and the western part of Ghazipur district), Azamgarh (Azamgarh district), and Mirzapur (Mirzapur, Sant Ravidas Nagar, and Bhadohi districts) in Uttar Pradesh. Banarasi is a local name for Bhojpuri, named after Baranas.[clarification needed] Other names for Western Bhojpuri include Purbi and Benarsi.[18]

Nagpuria Bhojpuri is the southernmost popular dialect, found in the Chota Nagpur Plateau of Jharkhand, particularly parts of Palamau and Ranchi. It has been influenced more by the Magahi language than by other dialects.[15][17] It is sometimes referred to as Sadari.[19]

A more specific classification recognises the dialects of Bhojpuri as Bhojpuri Tharu, Domra, Madhesi, Musahari, Northern Standard Bhojpuri (Basti, Gorakhpuri, Sarawaria), Southern Standard Bhojpuri (Kharwari), and Western Standard Bhojpuri (Benarsi, Purbi).[3]

Phonology[edit]

Vowels[20]

FrontCentralBack

Closei ɪu

Close-mideəo

Open-midɛɔ

Openæɑ

Consonants[20]

LabialDentalAlveolarRetroflex(Alveolo-)palatalVelarGlottal

Nasalmnɳɲŋ

Stopvoicelessptʈtɕk

voicedbdɖdʑg

aspiratedpʰtʰʈʰtɕʰkʰ

breathy voicedbɦdɦɖɦdʑɦgɦ

Fricativesh

Rhoticplainrɽ

aspiratedrɦɽɦ

Approximantw~ʋlj

Bhojpuri is, sociolinguistically, one of the seven Hindi languages (Haryanvi, Braj, Awadhi, Bhojpuri, Bundeli, Bagheli, and Kannauji).[8] Of the seven, Bhojpuri has the most allophonic variations in vowels.[21]

Bhojpuri has 6 vowel phonemes[22] and 10 vocoids. The higher vowels are relatively tense, and the lower vowels are relatively lax. The language has 31 consonant phonemes and 34 contoids (6 bilabial, 4 apico-dental, 5 apico-alveolar, 7 retroflex, 6 alveo-palatal, 5 dorso-velar, and 1 glottal).[20]

Linguist Robert L. Trammell published the phonology of Northern Standard Bhojpuri in 1971.[20][22] According to him, the syllable system is peak type: every syllable has the vowel phoneme as the highest point of sonority. Codas may consist of one, two, or three consonants. Vowels occur as simple peaks or as peak nuclei in diphthongs. The intonation system involves 4 pitch levels and 3 terminal contours.[20][23]

Writing system[edit]

Bhojpuri story written in Kaithi script by Babu Rama Smaran Lal in 1898

Bhojpuri was historically written in Kaithi script,[3] but since 1894 Devanagari has served as the primary script. Kaithi is now rarely used for Bhojpuri.

The word Bhojpuri written in Kaithi script

Kaithi script was used for administrative purposes in the Mughal era for writing Bhojpuri, Awadhi, Maithili, Magahi, and Hindustani from at least the 16th century up to the first decade of the 20th century. Government gazetteers[who?] report that Kaithi was used in a few districts of Bihar throughout the 1960s. Bhojpuri residents of India who moved to British colonies in Africa, the Indian Ocean, and the Caribbean in the 19th and early 20th centuries used both Kaithi and Devanagari scripts.[9]

Signboard at Purbi Gumti Arrah along with Persian script (on the right side) and Roman script (above). "Lock no. 11" is written on the board in Bhojpuri.

By 1894 both Kaithi and Devanagari became common scripts to write official texts in Bihar. At present almost all Bhojpuri texts are written in Devanagari, even in islands outside of India where Bhojpuri is spoken. In Mauritius, Kaithi script was historically considered informal, and Devanagari was sometimes spelled as Devanagri. In modern Mauritius, the major script is Devanagari.[24]

Politeness[edit]

Bhojpuri syntax and vocabulary reflects a three-tier system of politeness. Any verb can be conjugated through these tiers. The verb to come in Bhojpuri is aana, and the verb to speak is bolna. The imperatives come! and speak! can be conjugated in five ways, each marking subtle variation in politeness and propriety. These permutations exclude a host of auxiliary verbs and expressions, which can be added to verbs to add another degree of subtle variation. For extremely polite or formal situations, the pronoun is generally omitted.

Literary[teh] āō[teh] bōl

Casual and intimate[tu] āō[tu] bōl

Polite and intimate[tum] āv'[tum] bōl'

Formal yet intimate[rau'ā] āīñ[rau'ā] bōlīñ

Polite and formal[āpne] āīñ[āp] bōlīñ

Extremely formalāwal jā'ebōlal jā'e

Similarly, adjectives are marked for politeness and formality. The adjective your has several forms with different tones of politeness: tum (casual and intimate), "tōhār" (polite and intimate), "t'hār" (formal yet intimate), rā'ur (polite and formal), and āpke (extremely formal). Although there are many tiers of politeness, Bhojpuri speakers mainly use the form tum to address a younger individual and aap for an individual who is older, or holds a higher position in workplace situations.

Status[edit]

Greater official recognition of Bhojpuri, such as by inclusion in the Eighth Schedule to the Constitution of India, has been demanded.[by whom?][25] In 2018, Bhojpuri was given second-language status in Jharkhand state of India.[26] It is an official language in Nepal, and Fiji as Fiji Hindi.

Bhojpuri is taught in matriculation and at the higher secondary level in the Bihar School Education Board and the Board of High School and Intermediate Education Uttar Pradesh.[citation needed] It is also taught in various universities in India, such as Veer Kunwar Singh University,[27] Banaras Hindu University,[28] Nalanda Open University,[29] and Dr. Shakuntala Misra National Rehabilitation University.[30]

Literature[edit]

Main article: Bhojpuri literature

Lorikayan, the story of Veer Lorik contains Bhojpuri folklore from Eastern Uttar Pradesh.[31] Bhikhari Thakur's Bidesiya is a play, written as a book. Phool Daliya is a well-known book by Prasiddh Narayan Singh. It comprises poems of veer ras (A style of writing) on the theme of azaadi (Freedom) about his experiences in the Quit India movement and India's struggle with poverty after the country gained independence.

Media[edit]

Many Bhojpuri magazines and papers are published in Bihar, Jharkhand, and Uttar Pradesh. Several Bhojpuri newspapers are available locally in North India; they are not wealthy enough to be published online. Parichhan is a contemporary literary-cultural Maithili-Bhojpuri magazine, published by a Maithili-Bhojpuri academy and the government of Delhi, and edited by Parichay Das. The Sunday Indian, Bhojpuri[32] is a regular national news magazine in Bhojpuri. Aakhar is a monthly online Bhojpuri literature magazine.[33] Other media in Bhojpuri include Lok Lucknow,[34] and the channels Mahuaa TV and Hamar TV.

Common words[edit]

Weekdays[edit]

EnglishBhojpuri (Latin script)??????? (????? ?????: Kaithi)भोजपुरी (देवनागरी लिपि; Devanagari script)

SundayEitwaar?????एतवार

MondaySomaar?????सोमार

TuesdayMangar?????मंगर

WednesdayBudhh???बुध

ThursdayBifey?????बयिफे

FridaySook???सूक्र

SaturdaySanichar?????सनिचर

Common phrases[edit]

EnglishBhojpuri??????? (????? ?????: Kaithiभोजपुरी

HelloRaam Raam / Parnaam??? ???/ ?????राम राम / परणाम

Welcome/Please come inAain na??? ??आईं ना

How are you?Ka haal ba? / kaisan hava??? ??? ???/???? ??ऽ?का हाल बा? / कइसन हवऽ?

I'm good. And you?Hum theek baani. Aur rauwa? / Hum theek hain Aur aap??? ??? ???????? ????? /?? ??? ???? ??? ???हम ठीक बानी। अउर रउवा? / हम ठीक हऽ‍ी अउर आप?

What is your name?Tohaar naav ka ha? / Raur naav ka ha?????? ???? ?? ?ऽ?/???? ???? ?? ?ऽ?तोहार नाँव का ह? / राउर नाँव का ह?

My name is ...Hamar naav ... ha???? ???? ... ?ऽहमार नाँव ... ह

What's up?Kaa hot aa??? ?????का होताऽ?

I love youHum tohse pyaar kare ni / Hum tohra se pyaar kare ni?? ??? ?? ????? ?????/ ?? ????? ?? ????? ?????हम तोहसे प्यार करे नी / हम तोहरा से प्यार करे नी

Bhojpuri cinema, Bhojiwood or Bhollywood refers to the Indian Bhojpuri language film industry based in Bihar, India.[1]

The first Bhojpuri talkie film, Ganga Maiyya Tohe Piyari Chadhaibo, was released in 1963 by Vishwanath Shahabadi. The 80s saw the release of many notable as well as run-of-the-mill Bhojpuri films like Bitia Bhail Sayan, Chandwa ke take Chakor, Hamar Bhauji, Ganga Kinare Mora Gaon and Sampoorna Tirth Yatra. Bhojpuri cinema has grown in recent years. The Bhojpuri film industry is now a ?2000 crore industry.[2] Bhojpuri movies are seen across various parts of North America, Europe, and Asia where second and third generation migrants still speak the language, as well as in Guyana, Trinidad and Tobago, Suriname, Fiji, Mauritius, and South Africa, which has a large Bhojpuri population.[3]

Contents

1Overview

2History

3Notable people

3.1Film producers

3.2Film directors

3.3Actors

3.4Actresses

3.5Singers

4Notable films

5Awards

6See also

7Notes

8References

Overview[edit]

Bhojpuri, often considered a dialect of Hindi, originates in western Bihar and eastern Uttar Pradesh in northern India. Speakers of it and its creoles are found in many parts of the world, including the United States, the United Kingdom, Fiji, Guyana, Mauritius, South Africa, Suriname, and Trinidad and Tobago, and The Netherlands. During the late 1800s and early 1900s, many colonizers faced labor shortages due to the abolition of slavery; thus, they imported many Indians, many from Bhojpuri-speaking regions, as indentured servants to labor on plantations. Today, some 200 million people in the Caribbean, Oceania, and North America who speak Bhojpuri as a native or second language.[4]

History[edit]

In the 1960s, the first president of India, Rajendra Prasad, who hailed from Bihar, met Bollywood actor Nazir Hussain and asked him to make a movie in Bhojpuri, which eventually led to the release of the first Bhojpuri film in 1963.[5] Bhojpuri cinema's history begins with the well-received film Ganga Maiyya Tohe Piyari Chadhaibo ("Mother Ganges, I will offer you a yellow sari"), which was produced by Biswanath Prasad Shahabadi under the banner of Nirmal Pictures and directed by Kundan Kumar.[6] Throughout the following decades, films were produced in fits and starts. Bidesiya ("Foreigner", 1963, directed by S. N. Tripathi) and Ganga ("Ganges", 1965, directed by Kundan Kumar) were profitable and popular, but in general Bhojpuri films were not commonly produced in the 1960s and 1970s.

In the 1980s, enough Bhojpuri films were produced to tentatively make up an industry. Films such as Mai ("Mom", 1989, directed by Rajkumar Sharma) and Hamar Bhauji ("My Brother's Wife", 1983, directed by Kalpataru) continued to have at least sporadic success at the box office. Nadiya Ke Paar is a 1982 Hindi-Bhojpuri blockbuster directed by Govind Moonis and starring Sachin, Sadhana Singh, Inder Thakur, Mitali, Savita Bajaj, Sheela David, Leela Mishra and Soni Rathod. However, this trend faded out by the end of the decade. By 1990, the nascent industry seemed to be completely finished.[7]

The industry took off again in 2001 with the Silver Jubilee hit Saiyyan Hamar ("My Sweetheart", directed by Mohan Prasad), which shot its hero, Ravi Kissan, to superstardom.[8] This was quickly followed by several other remarkably successful films, including Panditji Batai Na Biyah Kab Hoi ("Priest, tell me when I will marry", 2005, directed by Mohan Prasad) and Sasura Bada Paisa Wala ("My father-in-law, the rich guy", 2005). In a measure of the Bhojpuri film industry's rise, both of these did much better business in the states of Bihar and Uttar Pradesh than mainstream Bollywood hits at the time. Both films, made on extremely tight budgets, earned back more than ten times their production costs.[9] Sasura Bada Paisa Wala introduced Manoj Tiwari, formerly a well-loved folk singer, to the wider audiences of Bhojpuri cinema. In 2008, he and Ravi Kissan were the leading actors of Bhojpuri films, and their fees increase with their fame. The extremely rapid success of their films has led to dramatic increases in Bhojpuri cinema's visibility, and the industry now supports an awards show[10] and a trade magazine, Bhojpuri City,[11] which chronicles the production and release of what are now over 100 films per year.

Many of the major stars of mainstream Bollywood cinema, including Amitabh Bachchan, have recently worked in Bhojpuri films. Mithun Chakraborty's Bhojpuri debut Bhole Shankar, released in 2008, is considered the biggest Bhojpuri hit of all time.[12] Also in 2008, a 21-minute diploma Bhojpuri film by Siddharth Sinha, Udedh Bun (Unravel) was selected for world premiere at the Berlin International Film Festival.[13] Later it won the National Film Award for Best Short fiction Film.[14][15]

Bhojpuri poet Manoj Bhawuk has written a history of Bhojpuri cinema.[16] Bhawuk is widely known as "Encyclopedia of Bhojpuri Cinema".

In February 2011, a three-day film and cultural festival in Patna marking 50 years of Bhojpuri cinema, opened Ganga Maiyya Tohe Piyari Chadhaibo the first Bhojpuri film. The first Bhojpuri Reality Film "Dhokha" is under production under banner Om Kaushik Films is about to be nominated and screened in different International Film Festivals under direction Of Rashmi Raj Kaushik Vicky and Renu Chaudhary.[17]

History of Bihar
From Wikipedia, the free encyclopedia
Jump to navigationJump to search
Outline of South Asian history
Palaeolithic (2,500,000–250,000 BC)[show]
Neolithic (10,800–3300 BC)[show]
Chalcolithic (3500–1500 BC)[show]
Bronze Age (3300–1300 BC)[show]
Iron Age (1500–200 BC)[show]
Middle Kingdoms (230 BC – AD 1206)[show]
Late medieval period (1206–1526)[show]
Early modern period (1526–1858)[show]
Colonial states (1510–1961)[show]
Periods of Sri Lanka[show]
National histories[show]
Regional histories[show]
Specialised histories[show]
v
t
e

The history of Bihar is one of the most varied in India. Bihar consists of three distinct regions, each has its own distinct history and culture. They are Magadh, Mithila and Bhojpur.[1] Chirand, on the northern bank of the Ganga River, in Saran district, has an archaeological record from the Neolithic age (about 2500–1345BC).[2][3] Regions of Bihar—such as Magadha, Mithila and Anga—are mentioned in religious texts and epics of ancient India. Mithila is believed to be the centre of Indian power in the Later Vedic period (c. 1100-500 BCE). Mithila first gained prominence after the establishment of the Videha kingdom.[4] The Kings of the Videha Kingdom where called Janakas. A daughter of one of the Janaks of Mithila, Sita, is mentioned as consort of Lord Rama in the Hindu epic Ramayana, written by Valmiki.[5] The Videha Kingdom later became incorporated into the Vajji confederacy which had its capital in the city of Vaishali, which is also in Mithila.[6]

Magadha, another region of Bihar was the centre of Indian power, learning and culture for about a thousand years. One of India's greatest empires, the Maurya empire, as well as two major pacifist religions, Buddhism and Jainism, arose from the region that is now Bihar.[7] Magadha empires, most notably the Maurya and Gupta empires, unified large parts of the Indian subcontinent under their rule.[8] Their capital Pataliputra, adjacent to modern-day Patna, was an important political, military and economic centre of Indian civilisation during the ancient and classical periods of Indian history. Many ancient Indian texts, aside from religious epics, were written in ancient Bihar. The play Abhijñānaśākuntala was the most prominent.

The present-day region of Bihar overlaps with several pre-Mauryan kingdoms and republics, including Magadha, Anga and the Vajji confederation of Mithila. The latter was one of the world's earliest known republics and had existed in the region since before the birth of Mahavira (c. 599 BCE).[9][10] The classical Gupta dynasty of Bihar presided over a period of cultural flourishing and learning, known today as the Golden Age of India.

The Pala Empire also made their capital at Pataliputra once during Devapala's rule. After the Pala period, Bihar played a very small role in Indian history until the emergence of the Suri dynasty during the Medieval period in the 1540s. After the fall of the Suri dynasty in 1556, Bihar again became a marginal player in India and was the staging post for the British colonial Bengal Presidency from the 1750s and up to the war of 1857–58.[clarification needed] On 22 March 1912, Bihar was carved out as a separate province in the British Indian Empire. Since 1947 independence, Bihar has been an original state of the Indian Union.

Contents
1Prehistoric era
2Vedic Period (1700-600 BC)2.1Rigvedic period
2.1.1Northern black polished ware
2.2Late Vedic Kingdoms
2.2.1Anga Kingdom
2.2.2Videha (Mithila) Kingdom
2.2.3Magadha Kingdom
3Mahajanapadas
4The Magadha Empire
5Middle Kingdoms
6Medieval Period
7Mughal Empire
8British Raj
8.1British East India Company
8.2The British Raj
8.3Independence movement
9Post-Independence
10Timeline for Bihar
11See also
12Gallery
13Further reading
14References
Prehistoric era[edit]
See also: Timeline for Bihar
The earliest proof of human activity in Bihar is Mesolithic habitational remains at Munger.

Prehistoric rock paintings have been discovered in the hills of Kaimur, Nawada and Jamui. It was the first time that a Neolithic settlement was discovered in the thick of the alluvium, over the bank of the Ganges at Chirand.[11] The rock paintings depict a prehistoric lifestyle and natural environment. They depict the sun, the moon, stars, animals, plants, trees, and

rivers, and it is speculated that they represent love for nature. The paintings also highlight the daily life of the early humans in Bihar, including activities like hunting, running, dancing and walking.[12] The rock paintings in Bihar are not only identical to those in central and southern India but are also akin to those in Europe and Africa. The rock paintings of Spain's Alta Mira and France's Lascaux are almost identical to those found in Bihar.[13]

In 2017 bricks dated to mature Harappan period were discovered from the outskirts of the ancient city of Vaishali.[14][15] Any in depth research which may establish definite links between Indus Valley Civilization and

Bihar is yet to be conducted.

Vedic Period (1700-600 BC)[edit]

Kikata, predecessor of Magadha as shown in early vedic period map, but most of the scholars place it in South Bihar

Rigvedic period[edit]

Kikata was an ancient kingdom in what is now India, mentioned in the Vedas. It is believed that they were the forefathers of Magadhas because Kikata is used as synonym for Magadha in the later texts.[16] It probably lay to the south of Magadha Kingdom in a hilly landscape.[17] A section in the Rigveda (RV 3.53.14) refers to the Kīkaṭas (Hindi:कीकट), a tribe which most scholars have placed in present-day south western Bihar (Magadha) such as Weber and Zimmer [18] while some scholars such as Oldenburg and Hillebrandt dispute that. According to Puranic literature Kikata is placed near Gaya. It is described as extending from Caran-adri to Gridharakuta (vulture peak), Rajgir. Some scholar such as A. N. Chandra place Kikata in a hilly part of Indus valley based on argument that countries between magadh and indus valley are not mentioned such as kuru, kosala etc. Kikatas were said to be Anarya or non vedic people who didn't practice vedic rituals like soma, According to Sayana, Kikatas didn't perform worship, were infidels and nastikas. The leader of Kikatas has been called Pramaganda, a usurer.[19][20] It is unclear whether Kikatas were already present in Magadh during rigvedic period or they migrated there later.[21] Like Rigveda attributes of Kikatas, Atharvaveda also speaks about south eastern tribes like Magadhas and Angas as hostile tribe who lived on the borders of Brahmanical India.[22] Bhagvata Purana mentions about the birth of Buddha among Kikatas.[23]

Anga, Kosala, Videha and other kingdoms of the late Vedic period

Northern black polished ware[edit]

Urbanization in the gangetic plains began with the appearance of Northern black polished ware period and archaeologists trace the origin of this pottery in Magadh region of Bihar. The oldest dated site of NBWP is in Juafardih, Nalanda, which is carbon dated to 1200 BC.[24]

Late Vedic Kingdoms[edit]

Main articles: Magadha Kingdom, Videha Kingdom, and Anga Kingdom

See also: Brihadrathas dynasty and Pradyota dynasty

Further information: Jarasandha, Karna, Mahabharata, Ramayana, Sita, Puranas, Kuru (kingdom), and Anga

Anga Kingdom[edit]

Anga kingdom is described in the Mahabharata. Karna, a friend of Duryodhana, was the king of Anga.

Videha (Mithila) Kingdom[edit]

Videha is mentioned in both the Ramayana and the Mahabharata as comprising parts of Bihar and extending into small parts of Nepal. The Hindu goddess Sita is described as the princess of Videha, daughter of Raja Janak. The capital of Videha is believed to be either Janakpur (in Present-day Nepal),[25] or Baliraajgadh (in Present-day Madhubani district, Bihar, India).[26][27]

Expansion of the Magadha state in the 6th-4th centuries BCE.

Magadha Kingdom[edit]

The Magadha was established by semi-mythical king Jarasandha, who the Puranas state was a king of the Brihadrathas dynasty and one of the descendants of King Puru. Jarasandha appears in the Mahabharatha as the "Magadhan Emperor who rules all India" and meets with an unceremonious ending. Jarasandha was the greatest among them during epic times. His capital, Rajagriha or Rajgir, is now a modern hill resort in Bihar. Jarasandha's continuous assault on the Yadava kingdom of Surasena resulted in their withdrawal from central India to western India. Jarasandha was a threat not only for the Yadavas but also for the Kurus. Pandava Bhima killed him in a mace dual aided by the intelligence of Vasudeva Krishna.

Thus, Yudhishthira, the Pandava King, could complete his campaign of bringing the whole of India into his empire. Jarasandha had friendly relations with Chedi king Shishupala, Kuru king Duryodhana and Anga king Karna. His descendants, according to the Vayu Purana, ruled Magadha for 1000 years followed by the Pradyota dynasty, which ruled for 138 years from 799–684 BCE[contradictory]. However, there is insufficient evidence to prove the historicity of this claim. These rulers are nonetheless mentioned in the Hindu, Buddhist, and Jain texts. Palaka, the son of the Avanti king Pradyota, conquered Kaushambi, increasing the kingdom's power.

Mahajanapadas[edit]

Main articles: Mahajanapadas, History of Buddhism, and History of Jainism

See also: Siddhartha Gautama and Mahavira

Further information: Vajji and Vaishali (ancient city)

The Mahajanapadas era

Anga, Vajji and Magadha on map of the Mahajanapadas.

Copy of the seal excavated from Kundpur, Vaishali. The Brahmi letters on the seal means: Kundpur was in Vaishali. Prince Vardhaman (Mahavira) used this seal after the Judgement.

Gautama Buddha undertaking extreme ascetic practices before his enlightenment on the bank of river Phalgu in Bodh Gaya, Bihar.

Detail of a leaf with, The Birth of Mahavira (the 24th Jain Tirthankara), from the Kalpa Sutra, c. 1375–1400.

In the later Vedic Age, a number of small kingdoms or city states, dominated Magadha. Many of these states have been mentioned in Buddhist and Jaina literature as far back as 1000 BCE. By 500 BCE, sixteen monarchies and 'republics' known as the Mahajanapadas —Kasi, Kosala, Anga, Magadha, Vajji (or Vriji), Malla, Chedi, Vatsa (or Vamsa), Kuru, Panchala, Machcha (or Matsya), Surasena, Assaka, Avanti, Gandhara and Kamboja— stretched across the Indo-Gangetic plains from modern-day Afghanistan to Bengal and Maharashtra. Vajji covered the modern North Bihar, Magadha covered South-western Bihar while Anga covered South-eastern Bihar. Many of the sixteen kingdoms had coalesced to four major ones by 500/400 BCE, that is by the time of Siddhartha Gautama. These four were Vatsa, Avanti, Kosala and Magadha.[28] In 537 BCE, Siddhartha Gautama attained the state of "enlightenment" in Bodh Gaya, Bihar. Around the same time, Mahavira who was born in a place called Kundalagrama in the ancient kingdom of Lachuar in Jamui District in modern-day Bihar. He was the 24th Jain Tirthankara, propagated a similar theology, that was to later become Jainism.[29] However, Jain orthodoxy believes it predates all known time. The Vedas are believed to have documented a few Jain Tirthankaras and an ascetic order similar to the sramana movement.[30] The Buddha's teachings and Jainism had doctrines inclined toward asceticism, and were preached in Prakrit, which helped them gain acceptance amongst the masses. They have profoundly influenced practices that Hinduism and Indian spiritual orders are associated with namely, vegetarianism, prohibition of animal slaughter and ahimsa (non-violence).

While the geographic impact of Jainism was limited to India, Buddhist nuns and monks eventually spread the teachings of Buddha to Central Asia, East Asia, Tibet, Sri Lanka and South East Asia. Nalanda University and Vikramshila University one of the oldest residential universities were established in Bihar during this period.

According to both Buddhist texts and Jain texts, one of Pradyota tradition was that king's son would kill his father to become the successor. During this time, it is reported that there was high crimes in Magadha. The people rose up and elected Shishunaga to become the new king, who destroyed the power of the Pradyotas and created the Shishunaga dynasty.

The Magadha Empire[edit]

Main article: Magadha

See also: Shishunaga dynasty, Nanda Dynasty, Mauryan dynasty, Shunga dynasty, and Kanva dynasty

Further information: Bimbisara, Ajatashatru, Mahapadma Nanda, Chandragupta Maurya, Bindusara, Ashoka, Samprati, and Pushyamitra Shunga

Further information: Kalinga War, Rajgriha, Pataliputra, Edicts of Ashoka, Ashokavadana, Arthashastra, and Emblem of India

Further information: Ambapali, Chanakya, and Brhadrata

Shishunaga (also called King Sisunaka) was the founder of a dynasty collectively called the Shishunaga dynasty. He established the Magadha empire (in 684 BCE). Due in part to this bloody dynastic feuding, it is thought that a civil revolt led to the emergence of the Shishunaga dynasty. This empire, with its original capital in Rajgriha, later shifted to Pataliputra (both currently in the Indian state of Bihar). The Shishunaga dynasty was one of the largest empires of the Indian subcontinent.

The Hariyanka dynasty king Bimbisara was responsible for expanding the boundaries of his kingdom through matrimonial alliances and conquest. The land of Kosala fell to Magadha in this way. Estimates place the territory ruled by this early dynasty at 300 leagues in diameter, and encompassing 80,000 small settlements. Bimbisara is contemporary with the Buddha, and is recorded as a lay disciple. Bimbisara (543–493 BCE) was imprisoned and killed by his own son who became his successor, Ajatashatru (491–461 BCE), under whose rule, the dynasty reached its largest extent.

Magadha

Bimbisara's jail, where King Bimbisara was imprisoned by his son Ajatashatru, in Rajgir

Ajatashatru's stupa in Rajgir, where his ashes were interred.

Vaishali was the capital of Vajjian Confederacy, believed to be the world's earliest republic.[10][31][32][33]

Ashokan Pillar at Vaishali.

Licchavi was an ancient—before the birth of Mahavira— republic in what is now the Bihar state of India.[10] Vaishali was the capital of Licchavi and the Vajjian Confederacy. The Mahavamsa tells that a courtesan in that city, Ambapali, was famous for her beauty, and helped in large measure in making the city prosperous.[34]

Ajatashatru went to war with the Licchavi several times. Ajatashatru is thought to have ruled from 551 BCE to 519 BCE and moved the capital of the Magadha kingdom from Rajagriha to Pataliputra. The Mahavamsa tells that Udayabhadra eventually succeeded his father, Ajatashatru, and that under him Pataliputra became the largest city in the world. He is thought to have ruled for sixteen years. The kingdom had a particularly bloody succession. Anuruddha eventually succeeded Udaybhadra through assassination, and his son Munda succeeded him in the same fashion, as did his son Nagadasaka.

The Nanda Empire at its greatest extent under Dhana Nanda c. 323 BCE.

This dynasty lasted until 424 BCE, when it was overthrown by the Nanda dynasty. This period saw the development in Magadha of two of India's major religions. Gautama Buddha in the 6th or 5th century BCE was the founder of Buddhism, which later spread to East Asia and Southeast Asia, while Mahavira revived and propagated the ancient sramanic religion of Jainism.

The Nanda dynasty was established by an illegitimate son of King Mahanandin from the previous Shishunaga dynasty. The Nanda dynasty ruled Magadha during the 5th and 4th centuries BC. At its greatest extent, the Nanda Empire extended from Burma in the east, Balochistan in the west and probably as far south as Karnataka.[35] Mahapadma Nanda of Nanda dynasty, has been described as the destroyer of all the Kshatriyas. He defeated the Ikshvaku dynasty, as well as the Panchalas, Kasis, Haihayas, Kalingas, Asmakas, Kurus, Maithilas, Surasenas and the Vitihotras. He expanded his territory to the south of Deccan. Mahapadma Nanda died at the age of 88 and, therefore, he ruled during most of the period of this dynasty, which lasted 100 years.

The Maurya Empire at its largest extent under Ashoka the Great.

Silver punch mark coin of the Maurya empire, with symbols of wheel and elephant. 3rd century BC.

In 321 BC, exiled general Chandragupta Maurya, with the help of Chanakya, founded the Maurya dynasty after overthrowing the reigning Nanda king Dhana Nanda to establish the Maurya Empire. The Maurya Empire (322–185 BC), ruled by the Mauryan dynasty, was geographically extensive, powerful and a political-military empire in ancient India. During this time, most of the subcontinent was united under a single government for the first time. The exceptions were present day Tamil Nadu and Kerala (which was a Tamil kingdom at that time). The empire had its capital city at Pataliputra (near modern Patna). The Mauryan empire under Chandragupta Maurya would not only conquer most of the Indian subcontinent, defeating and conquering the satraps left by Alexander the Great, but also push its boundaries into Persia and Central Asia, conquering the Gandhara region. Chandragupta Maurya then defeated an invasion led by Seleucus I, a Greek general from Alexander's army. Chandragupta Maurya's minister, Kautilya Chanakya, wrote the Arthashastra, a treatise on economics, politics, foreign affairs, administration, military arts, war and religion.

Chandragupta Maurya was succeeded by his son, Bindusara, who expanded the kingdom over most of present-day India, other than the extreme south and east. At its greatest extent, the Empire stretched to the north along the natural boundaries of the Himalayas, and to the east stretching into what is now Assam. To the west, it reached beyond modern Pakistan, annexing Balochistan and much of what is now Afghanistan. The Empire was extended into India's central and southern regions by the emperors Chandragupta and Bindusara, but it excluded the republic of Kalinga.

The Maurya Empire was inherited by Bindusara's son, Ashoka. Ashoka initially sought to expand his kingdom but in the aftermath of the carnage caused during the invasion of Kalinga, he renounced bloodshed and pursued a policy of non-violence or ahimsa after converting to Buddhism. Following the conquest of Kalinga, Ashoka ended the military expansion of the empire, and led the empire through more than 40 years of relative peace, harmony and prosperity. Ashoka's response to the Kalinga War is recorded in the Edicts of Ashoka,[36] one of the oldest preserved historical documents of the Indian subcontinent.[37][38][39]

Mauryan Sculptures

According to Rock Edicts of Ashoka:

Beloved-of-the-Gods [Ashoka], King Priyadarsi, conquered the Kalingas eight years after his coronation. 150000 were deported, 100000 were killed and much more died (from other causes). After the Kalingas had been conquered, Beloved-of-the-Gods came to feel a strong inclination towards the Dhamma, a love for the Dhamma and for instruction in Dhamma. Now Beloved-of-the-Gods feels deep remorse for having conquered the Kalingas.

— Ashoka, S. Dhammika, The Edicts of King Ashoka, Kandy, Buddhist Publications Society (1994) ISBN 955-24-0104-6

The Mauryan Empire under Ashoka was responsible for the proliferation of Buddhist ideals across the whole of East Asia and South-East Asia. Under Ashoka, India was a prosperous and stable empire of great economic and military power whose political influence and trade extended across Asia and into Europe. Chandragupta Maurya's embrace of Jainism increased social and religious renewal and reform across his society, while Ashoka embraced Buddhism. Ashoka sponsored the spreading of Buddhist ideals into Sri Lanka and South-East Asia. The Lion Capital of Ashoka at Sarnath, is the emblem of India. Archaeologically, the period of Mauryan rule in South Asia falls into the era of Northern Black Polished Ware (NBPW). The Arthashastra, the Edicts of Ashoka and Ashokavadana are primary sources of written records of the Mauryan times.

The Shunga Empire at its greatest extent -c. 185 BCE

Ashoka was followed for 50 years by a succession of weaker kings. Brihadrata, the last ruler of the Mauryan dynasty, held territories that had shrunk considerably from the time of emperor Ashoka, although he still upheld the Buddhist faith. The Shunga dynasty was established in 185 BC, about fifty years after Ashoka's death, when the king Brihadratha, the last of the Mauryan rulers, was assassinated by the then commander-in-chief of the Mauryan armed forces, Pushyamitra Shunga.

Pushyamitra Shunga was a Brahmin who then took over the throne and established the Shunga dynasty. Buddhist records such as the Ashokavadana write that the assassination of Brihadrata and the rise of the Shunga empire led to a wave of persecution of Buddhists,[40] and a resurgence of Hinduism. According to John Marshall,[41] Pushyamitra Shunga may have been the main author of the persecutions, although later Shunga kings seem to have been more supportive of Buddhism. Other historians, such as Etienne Lamotte[42] and Romila Thapar,[43] partially support this view.

Middle Kingdoms[edit]

Main articles: Gupta Empire and Pala Empire

Gupta Coins

Gold Coin of Samudragupta, with Garuda pillar, British Museum

Gold coin of Chandragupta II with horse, British Museum.

Gold coin of depicting Kumaragupta I Mahendraditya (414–455 CE) fighting with lion.

The Gupta Empire had their capital at Pataliputra

Aryabhata came to Kusumapura (modern Patna) for higher studies and lived here.[44] (PictureStatue of Aryabhata at IUCAA)

Kalidasa's Sanskrit play Abhijñānaśākuntala is one of the legacies of the Gupta Empire.

The Gupta dynasty ruled from around 240 to 550 CE. The origins of the Gupta Dynasty are shrouded in obscurity. The Chinese traveller Xuanzang provides the first evidence of the Gupta kingdom in Magadha. He came to India in 672 CE and heard of 'Maharaja Sri-Gupta' who built a temple for Chinese pilgrims near Mrigasikhavana. Ghatotkacha (c. 280–319) CE, had a son named Chandra Gupta I (Not to be confused with Chandragupta Maurya (340–293 BC), founder of the Mauryan Empire). In a breakthrough deal, Chandra Gupta I was married to a woman from Lichchhavi—the main power in Magadha.

Samudragupta succeeded Chandra Gupta I in 335, and ruled for about 45 years, until his death in 380. He attacked the kingdoms of Shichchhatra, Padmavati, Malwas, the Yaudheyas, the Arjunayanas, the Maduras and the Abhiras, and merged them in his kingdom. By his death in 380, he had incorporated over twenty kingdoms into his realm, his rule extended from the Himalayas to the river Narmada and from the Brahmaputra to the Yamuna. He gave himself the titles King of Kings and World Monarch. He is considered the Napoleon of India. Chandra Gupta I performed Ashwamedha Yajna to underline the importance of his conquest.

Chandra Gupta II, the Sun of Power (Vikramaditya), ruled from 380 until 413. Only marginally less successful than his father, Chandra Gupta II expanded his realm westwards, defeating the Saka Western Kshatrapas of Malwa, Gujarat and Saurashtra in a campaign lasting until 409. Chandragupta II was succeeded by his son Kumaragupta I. Known as the Mahendraditya, he ruled until 455. Towards the end of his reign a tribe in the Narmada valley, the Pushyamitras, rose in power to threaten the empire.

Skandagupta is generally considered the last of the great rulers.[45] He defeated the Pushyamitra threat, but then was faced with invading Hephthalites or Huna, from the northwest. He repulsed a Huna attack c. 477. Skandagupta died in 487 and was succeeded by his son Narasimhagupta Baladitya.

The Gupta Empire was one of the largest political and military empires in ancient India. The Gupta period is referred to as the Classical age of India by most historians. The time of the Gupta Empire was an "Indian Golden Age" in Indian science, technology, engineering, art, dialectic, literature, logic, mathematics, astronomy, religion and philosophy.[46]

The Gupta Empire had their capital at Pataliputra. The difference between Gupta Empire's and Mauryan Empire's administration was that in the Mauryan administration power was centralised but in the Gupta administration power was more decentralised. The empire was divided into provinces and the provinces were further divided into districts. Villages were the smallest units. The kingdom covered Gujarat, North-East India, south-eastern Pakistan, Odisha, northern Madhya Pradesh and eastern India with capital at Pataliputra, modern Patna. All forms of worship were carried out in Sanskrit.

Rapid strides were made in astronomy during this period. Aryabhata and Varahamihira were two great astronomers and mathematicians. Aryabhata stated that the earth moved round the sun and rotated on its own axis. Aryabhata, who is believed to be the first to come up with the concept of zero, postulated the theory that the Earth moves round the Sun, and studied solar and lunar eclipses. Aryabhata's most famous work was Aryabhatiya. Varahamihira's most important contributions are the encyclopaedic Brihat-Samhita and Pancha-Siddhantika (Pañcasiddhāntikā). Metallurgy also made rapid strides. The proof can be seen in the Iron Pillar of Vaishali[47] and near Mehrauli on the outskirts of Delhi, which was brought from Bihar.[48]

This period is also very rich in Sanskrit literature. The material sources of this age were Kalidasa's works. Raghuvamsa, Malavikagnimitram, Meghadūta, Abhijñānaśākuntala and Kumārasambhava, Mrichchakatika by Shudraka, Sharma, Kama Sutra (the principles of pleasure) and 13 plays by Bhasa were also written in this period.

In medicine, the Guptas were notable for their establishment and patronage of free hospitals. Although progress in physiology and biology was hindered by religious injunctions against contact with dead bodies, which discouraged dissection and anatomy, Indian physicians excelled in pharmacopoeia, caesarean section, bone setting, and skin grafting. Indeed, Hindu medical advances were soon adopted in the Arab and Western worlds. Ayurveda was the main medical system.

According to some historian's work,

The Gupta Empire is considered by many scholars to be the "classical age" of Hindu and Buddhist art and literature. The Rulers of the Gupta Empire were strong supporters of developments in the arts, architecture, science, and literature. The Gupta Empire circulated a large number of gold coins, called dinars, with their inscriptions. The Gupta Dynasty also left behind an effective administrative system. During times of peace, the Gupta Empire system was decentralised, with only taxation flowing to the capital at Pataliputra. During times of war however, the government realigned and fought its invaders. The system was soon extinguished in fighting off the Hunnic Invasions.[49][50]

Nalanda is considered one of the first great universities in recorded history. It was the centre of Buddhist learning and research in the world from 450 to 1193 CE. It reached its height under the Palas.

The Pala Empire was a Buddhist dynasty that ruled from the Bengal region of the Indian subcontinent. The name Pala (Modern Bengali: পাল pal) means protector and was used as an ending to the names of all Pala monarchs. The Palas were followers of the Mahayana and Tantric schools of Buddhism. Gopala was the first ruler from the dynasty. He came to power in 750 in Gaur by a democratic election. This event is recognised as one of the first democratic elections in South Asia since the time of the Mahā Janapadas. He reigned from 750-770 and consolidated his position by extending his control over all of Bengal as well as parts of Bihar. The Buddhist dynasty lasted for four centuries (750-1120 CE).

The empire reached its peak under Dharmapala and Devapala. Dharmapala extended the empire into the northern parts of the Indian Subcontinent. This triggered once again the power struggle for the control of the subcontinent. Devapala, successor of Dharmapala, expanded the empire to cover much of South Asia and beyond. His empire stretched from Assam and Utkala in the east, Kamboja (modern day Afghanistan) in the north-west and Deccan in the south. According to Pala copperplate inscription, Devapala exterminated the Utkalas, conquered the Pragjyotisha (Assam), shattered the pride of the Huna, and humbled the lords of Pratiharas, Gurjara and the Dravidas.

The Palas created many temples and works of art as well as supported the Universities of Nalanda and Vikramashila. Both Nalanda University and Vikramshila University reached their peak under the Palas. The universities received an influx of students from many parts of the world. Bihar and Bengal were invaded by the south Indian Emperor Rajendra Chola I of the Chola dynasty in the 11th century.[51][52] The Pala Empire eventually disintegrated in the 12th century under the attack of the Sena dynasty. Pala Empire was the last empire of middle kingdoms whose capital was once in Pataliputra (modern Patna) under Devapala's rule.

Medieval Period[edit]

See also: Sher Shah Suri and Raja Horil Singh

Further information: Decline of Buddhism in India, Suri dynasty, Oiniwar Dynasty, and Kharagpur Raj

Medieval Period

Sher Shah Suri revived Bihar to position of glory.

The 10th Sikh Guru Gobind Singh was born in Patna, Bihar.

A view of Takht Shri Harmandir Saheb, Patna.

Bihar was largely in ruins when visited by Xuanzang, the famous Buddhist monk from China, and suffered further damage at the hands of Muslim raiders in the 12th century.[53] With the advent of the foreign aggression and eventual foreign subjugation of India, Bihar passed through very uncertain times during the medieval period. Muhammad of Ghor attacked this region of the Indian subcontinent many times. Muhammad of Ghor's armies destroyed many Buddhist structures, including the great Nalanda university.[54]

The Buddhism of Magadha was finally swept away by the Islamic invasion under Muhammad Bin Bakhtiar Khilji, one of Qutb-ud-Din's generals destroyed monasteries fortified by the Sena armies, during which many of the viharas and the famed universities of Nalanda and Vikramshila were destroyed, and thousands of Buddhist monks were massacred in the 12th century.[55][56][57][58][59]

After fall of Pala empire, the Chero dynasty ruled some parts of Bihar from 12th century to 16th century till Mughal rule.[60]

Medieval Bihar saw a period of glory lasting about six years during the rule of Sher Shah Suri, who hailed from Sasaram. Sher Shah Suri built the longest road of the Indian subcontinent, the Grand Trunk Road, which started at Calcutta (Bengal) and ended at Peshawar, now Pakistan. The economic reforms carried out by Sher Shah, such as the introduction of the Rupee and Custom Duties, are still used in the Republic of India. He revived the city of Patna, where he built his headquarters.[61][62]

Hemu, the Hindu Emperor, the son of a food seller, and himself a vendor of saltpetre at Rewari,[63] rose to become Chief of Army and Prime Minister[64][65] under the command of Adil Shah Suri of the Suri Dynasty. He had won 22 battles against the Afghans, from Punjab to Bengal and had defeated Akbar's forces twice, at Agra and Delhi in 1556,[66] before succeeding to the throne of Delhi and establishing a 'Hindu Raj' in North India, albeit for a short duration, from Purana Quila in Delhi. He was killed in the Second Battle of Panipat.

Mughal Empire[edit]

See also: Zamindars of Bihar

In 1576, after the Battle of Tukaroi, Mughal Emperor Akbar the Great conquered Bengal Sultanate and added it to his empire domain. He divided Bihar and Bengal each into one of his original twelve subahs (imperial top-level provinces; Bihar with seat at Patna) and the region passed through uneventful provincial rule during much of this period. Bihar was left under Mughal control until the Battle of Plassey in 1757.[67]

After 182 years of Mughal control, Bihar passed into the control of Nawabs of Bengal under British suzernity. This period saw Bihar's exploitation at the hands of the rulers in the form of high taxes, but the Nawabs of Bengal also allowed trade to flourish in the region. Some of the greatest melas of the Indian subcontinent, such as the Soenpur Mela, which was the biggest cattle fair in India, were allowed to continue and even flourish with traders coming from near and far.

Prince Azim-us-Shan, the grandson of Aurangzeb was appointed as the governor of Bihar in 1703.[68] Azim-us-Shan renamed Pataliputra or Patna as Azimabad, in 1704.[69][70]

British Raj[edit]

British East India Company[edit]

See also: Veer Kunwar Singh, Siege of Arrah, and Battle of Chatra

Veer Kunwar Singh, during India's First War of Independence in 1857, he led a select band of armed soldiers against the troops under the command of the British East India Company.

After the Battle of Buxar, 1764, which was fought in Buxar, hardly 115 km from Patna, the Mughals as well as the Nawabs of Bengal lost effective control over the territories then constituting the province of Bengal, which currently comprises Bangladesh and the Indian states of West Bengal, Bihar, Jharkhand, Odisha. The British East India Company was accorded the diwani rights, that is, the right to administer the collection and management of revenues of the province of Bengal, and parts of Oudh, currently comprising a large part of Uttar Pradesh. The diwani rights were legally granted by Shah Alam, who was then the sovereign Mughal emperor of India. During the rule of the British East India Company in Bihar, Patna emerged as one of the most important commercial and trading centres of eastern India, preceded only by Kolkata.

Babu Kunwar Singh of Jagdishpur and his army, as well as countless other persons from Bihar, contributed to the India's First War of Independence (1857), also called the Sepoy Mutiny by some historians. Babu Kunwar Singh (1777–1858) one of the leaders of the Indian uprising of 1857 belonged[71] to a royal Rajput house of Jagdispur, currently a part of Bhojpur district of Bihar. By that time Bihar had many feudal estates or Zamindars. Most notably Tekari Raj, Raj Darbhanga, Tajpur Estate, Mohrampur Jagir, Bettiah Raj, Hathwa Raj, Kharagpur Raj and Banaili Estate. At the age of 80 years, during India's First War of Independence, he actively led a select band of armed soldiers against the troops under the command of the East India Company, and also recorded victories in many battles.[72]

The British Raj[edit]

Under the British Raj, Bihar particularly Patna gradually started to attain its lost glory and emerged as an important and strategic centre of learning and trade in India. From this point, Bihar remained a part the Bengal Presidency of the British Raj until 1912, when the province of Bihar and Orissa was carved out as a separate province. When the Bengal Presidency was partitioned in 1912 to carve out a separate province, Patna was made the capital of the new province. The city limits were stretched westwards to accommodate the administrative base, and the township of Bankipore took shape along the Bailey Road (originally spelt as Bayley Road, after the first Lt. Governor, Charles Stuart Bayley). This area was called the New Capital Area. The houses of the English residents, were all at the west-end at Bankipore. The greater part of the English residences were on the banks of the river, many of them being on the northern side of an open square, which formed the parade ground, and racecourse (present Gandhi Maidan). There was also the Golghar a wondrous bell-shaped building, one hundred feet high, with a winding outer staircase leading to the top, and a small entrance door at the base, which was intended for a granary, to be filled when there was the expectation of famine. It was initially considered to be both politically and materially impracticable.

(Sitting L to R) Deshratna Dr.Rajendra Prasad and Bihar Vibhuti Anugrah Narayan Sinha during Mahatma Gandhi's 1917 Champaran Satyagraha

To this day, locals call the old area as the City whereas the new area is called the New Capital Area. The Patna Secretariat with its imposing clock tower and the Patna High Court are two imposing landmarks of this era of development. Credit for designing the massive and majestic buildings of colonial Patna goes to the architect, I. F. Munnings. By 1916-1917, most of the buildings were ready for occupation. These buildings reflect either Indo-Saracenic influence (like Patna Museum and the state Assembly), or overt Renaissance influence like the Raj Bhawan and the High Court. Some buildings, like the General Post Office (GPO) and the Old Secretariat bear pseudo-Renaissance influence. Some say, the experience gained in building the new capital area of Patna proved very useful in building the imperial capital of New Delhi.

The British built several educational institutions in Patna like Patna College, Patna Science College, Bihar College of Engineering, Prince of Wales Medical College and the Bihar Veterinary College. With government patronage, the Biharis quickly seized the opportunity to make these centres flourish quickly and attain renown. In 1935, certain portions of Bihar were reorganised into the separate province of Orissa. Patna continued as the capital of Bihar province under the British Raj.

Independence movement[edit]

Bihar played a major role in the Indian independence struggle. Most notable were the Champaran movement against the Indigo plantation and the Quit India Movement of 1942.

After his return from South Africa, it was from Bihar that Mahatma Gandhi launched his pioneering civil-disobedience movement, Champaran Satyagraha.[73] Raj Kumar Shukla drew Mahatma Gandhi's attention to the exploitation of the peasants by the European indigo planters. Champaran Satyagraha received the spontaneous support from many Biharis, including Brajkishore Prasad, Rajendra Prasad (who became the first President of India) and Anugrah Narayan Sinha (who became the first Deputy Chief Minister and Finance Minister of Bihar).[74]

In India's struggle for independence, the Champaran Satyagraha marks a very important stage. Raj Kumar Shukla drew the attention of Mahatma Gandhi, who had just returned from South Africa, to the plight of the peasants suffering under an oppressive system established by European indigo planters. Besides other excesses they were forced to cultivate indigo on 3/20 part of their holding and sell it to the planters at prices fixed by the planters. This marked Gandhi's entry into the India's independence movement. On arrival at the district headquarters in Motihari, Gandhi and his team of lawyers—Dr. Rajendra Prasad, Dr. Anugrah Narayan Sinha, Brajkishore Prasad and Ram Navami Prasad, who he had handpicked to participate in the satyagraha—were ordered to leave by the next available train. They refused to do this, and Gandhi was arrested. He was released and the ban order was withdrawn in the face of a "Satyagraha" threat. Gandhi conducted an open inquiry into the peasant's grievances. The Government had to appoint an inquiry committee with Gandhi as a member. This led to the abolition of the system.

Raj Kumar Shukla has been described by Gandhi in his Atmakatha, as a man whose suffering gave him the strength to rise against the odds. In his letter to Gandhi he wrote "Respected Mahatma, You hear the stories of others everyday. Today please listen to my story.... I want to draw your attention to the promise made by you in the Lucknow Congress that you would come to Champaran. The time has come for you to fulfill your promise. 1.9 million suffering people of Champaran are waiting to see you."

Gandhi reached Patna on 10 April 1917 and on 16 April he reached Motihari accompanied by Raj Kumar Shukla. Under Gandhi's leadership the historic "Champaran Satyagraha" began. The contribution of Raj Kumar Shukla is reflected in the writings of Dr. Rajendra Prasad, first President of India, Anugrah Narayan Sinha, Acharya Kriplani and Mahatma Gandhi. Raj Kumar Shukla maintained a diary in which he gave an account of struggle against the atrocities of the indigo planters, atrocities so movingly depicted by Dinabandhu Mitra in Nil Darpan, a play that was translated by Michael Madhusudan Dutt. This movement by Mahatma Gandhi received the spontaneous support of a cross section of people, including Dr. Rajendra Prasad, Bihar Kesari Sri Krishna Sinha, Dr. Anugrah Narayan Sinha and Brajkishore Prasad.

Shaheed Baikuntha Shukla was another nationalist from Bihar, who was hanged for murdering a government approver named Phanindrananth Ghosh. This led to the hanging of Bhagat Singh, Sukhdev and Rajguru. Phanindranath Ghosh hitherto a key member of the Revolutionary Party had betrayed the cause by turning an approver and giving evidence, which led to his murder. Baikunth was commissioned to plan the murder of Ghosh. He carried out the killing successfully on 9 November 1932. He was arrested, tried, convicted, and, on 14 May 1934, he was hanged in Gaya Central Jail.

In North and Central Bihar, a peasant movement was an important side effect of the independence movement. The Kisan Sabha movement started in Bihar under the leadership of Swami Sahajanand Saraswati who in 1929 had formed the Bihar Provincial Kisan Sabha (BPKS) to mobilise peasant grievances against the zamindari attacks on their occupancy rights.[75] Gradually the peasant movement intensified and spread across the rest of India. All these radical developments on the peasant front culminated in the formation of the All India Kisan Sabha (AIKS) at the Lucknow session of the Indian National Congress in April 1936, with Swami Sahajanand Saraswati elected as its first President.[76] This movement aimed at overthrowing the fedual zamindari system instituted by the British. It was led by Swami Sahajanand Saraswati and his followers Pandit Yamuna Karjee, Rahul Sankrityayan and others. Pandit Yamuna Karjee along with Rahul Sankrityayan and other Hindi literaries started publishing a Hindi weekly Hunkar from Bihar in 1940. Hunkar later became the mouthpiece of the peasant movement and the agrarian movement in Bihar and was instrumental in spreading the movement. The peasant movement later spread to other parts of the country and helped in digging out the British roots in the Indian society by overthrowing the zamindari system.

Bihar's contribution in the independence movement has been immense with famous leaders like Swami Sahajanand Saraswati,[77] Shaheed Baikuntha Shukla, Sri Krishna Singh (Sinha),Bihar Bibhuti Anugrah Narayan Sinha, Mulana Mazharul Haque, Loknayak Jayaprakash Narayan, Basawon Singh (Sinha), Yogendra Shukla, Sheel Bhadra Yajee, Pandit Yamuna Karjee, Dr. Maghfoor Ahmad Ajazi and many others who worked for India's indepdence and worked to lift up the underprivileged masses. Khudiram Bose, Upendra Narayan Jha "Azad" and Prafulla Chaki were also active in revolutionary movement in Bihar.

Towards the end of 1946, between 30 October and 7 November,a massacre of Muslims in Bihar made Partition more likely. Begun as a reprisal for the Noakhali riot,it was difficult for authorities to deal with because it was spread out over a large number of scattered villages, and the number of casualties was impossible to establish accurately: "According to a subsequent statement in the British Parliament, the death-toll amounted to 5,000. The Statesman's estimate was between 7,500 and 10,000; the Congress party admitted to 2,000; Mr. Jinnah claimed about 30,000."[78]

The first Cabinet of Bihar was formed on 2 April 1946, consisting of two members, Dr. Sri Krishna Sinha as the first Chief Minister of Bihar and Dr. Anugrah Narayan Sinha as Deputy Chief Minister and Finance Minister of Bihar (also in charge of Labour, Health, Agriculture and Irrigation).[79][80][81] Other ministers were inducted later. The Cabinet served as the first Bihar Government after independence in 1947. In 1950, Dr. Rajendra Prasad from Bihar became the first President of India.

Post-Independence[edit]

See also: 2008 attacks on North Indians in Maharashtra

The 1974 smallpox epidemic of India occurred primarily in Bihar and a few other Indian states, killing thousands of people. The state of Jharkhand was carved out of Bihar in the year 2000.[82] 2005 Bihar assembly elections ended the 15 years of continuous RJD rule in the state, giving way to NDA led by Nitish Kumar. Bihari migrant workers have faced violence and prejudice in many parts of India, like Maharashtra, Punjab and Assam.[83][84][85] To mark the separation of Bihar from Bengal on 22 March 1912, the completion of 100 years of existence is being celebrated in the name of Bihar Shatabadi Celebration Utsav.[86] There was a political crisis over post of the chief minister during February 2015.

Timeline for Bihar[edit]

2500–1345 BCE: Chirand, on the northern bank of the Ganga River, in Saran district, has an archaeological record from the Neolithic age.

1100-500 BCE: Mithila region of present-day Bihar became the centre of Indian power in the later Vedic Period during the rule of Janaks of Videha.[87]

560–480 BCE: The era of Buddha.

Around 500-around 300 BCE: Foundation and rule of world's first republic, Vajji, a confederation of various clans, in the Mithila region of present-day Bihar with capital at Vaishali and Lichhivis are the most powerful clan of Vajji.

490 BCE: Establishment of Pataliputra (Modern Patna).

Before 325 BCE: Nanda clan rules in Magadha.

450–362 BCE: Emperor Mahapadma Nanda is ruler of the Magadh Empire, Nanda Dynasty.

304 BCE: Ashok Maurya born in Pataliputra

325–185 BCE: Magadh Empire under the Maurya Dynasty

340 BCE: General Chandragupta Maurya crowned Emperor of Magadh; Chandragupta is the first Mauryan emperor.

273 BCE: Ashok Maurya crowned new Emperor of Magadh, Buddhism is exported to Persian Empire, Greece, China and East Asia

273–232: Majority of 'Indian' region brought under the control of the Magadh Empire by Ashoka-The Great.

232 BCE: Death of Emperor Ashok Maurya

250 BCE: 3rd Buddhist Council

185 BCE–80 CE: The Magadha Empire falls under the Shunga Dynasty after the military coup by General Pushyamitra Shunga.

71–26 BCE: Magadh Empire falls under the Kanva dynasty

240–600 CE: Magadh Empire falls under the Gupta Dynasty. First ruler is Chandra Gupta

375–415: Emperor Chandragupta II

500: Attack by Huns weakens the power of Guptas. Provinces break away from the Magadh Empire.

Around 6th century — 11th century : The rule of Pala and Sena dynastys in Mithila region.

600–650: Harsha Vardhana empire expands into Magadh from the present-day Haryana.

750–1200: The Pala Dynasty Expands into Magadh.

11th century- around 1325: The Karnata dynasty rules Mithila region.

1200: Bakhtiyar Khilji's army destroys the Buddhist universities at Nalanda and Vikramshila. Start of the Muslim Era.

1200–1400: Sharp decline of Buddhism in Bihar and northern India in general.

1250–1526: Magadh and Mithila regions come under the Delhi Sultanate.

1526–1540: Mughal Emperor, Babur, defeats the last Sultan of Delhi, Lodi, and establishes the Mughal Dynasty.

1540–1555: Shenshah SherShah Suri (from Sasaram, modern south Bihar) captures empire from Mughals (SherShah built the Grand Trunk Road, introduced the Rupee and Custom Duties).

1556: Hindu King Hem Chandra Vikramaditya popular as Hemu takes control of Agra and Delhi as a Vikramaditya King and declares Hindu rule in North India.

1556: Mughal dynasty regains control of Agra after the Battle of Panipat.

1556–1764: Bihar becomes a province of the Mughal Empire.

1666: Guru Gobind Singh The 10th and last Sikh Guru, is born in modern-day Patna.

1757–1857: The British East India Company expands it rule into Bihar from Bengal.

1764: Battle of Buxar, Core lands of Mughal-ruled Hindustan are put firmly under British Company government. Tax collection rights are now a duty of the Company.

1764–1920: Migration of Bihari & Eastern United Provinces (modern-day Eastern Uttar Pradesh) workers across the British Empire under the rule of the Company and later Crown Government. Bihari migrant population dominate and settle in Guyana, Surinam, Trinidad-Tobago, Fiji, Mauritius, and Natal-South Africa. Smaller number of migrants also settles in Jamaica.

1857: Period of the Revolution of 1857. East India Company Sepoys (80% Hindu according to William Daryample in the book "The Last Mughal") declare Bahadur Shah Zafar II Emperor of Hindustan. The region becomes the centre of resistance to the East India Company. End of the Muslim Era.

1858: Mughal Sultanate-e-Hind reorganised to form the new British Indian Empire after the British Government abolishes the East India Company. Start of the British Age

1877: House of Windsor is made the new Imperial Royal Family. Queen Victoria declared the first Empress of the British Indian Empire

1912: Province of Bihar and Orissa separated from Bengal

1913: Start of the dramatic slowdown in wealth creation throughout India including Bihar

1916: Patna High Court founded

1917: Mahatma Gandhi arrives in Champaran with a team of[88] eminent lawyers:[89] Brajkishore Prasad, Rajendra Prasad, Anugrah Narayan Sinha and others.[88] The Champaran Satyagraha movement is launched. Establishment of Patna University.

1925: Patna Medical College Hospital established under the name "Prince of Wales Medical College"

1935: 1935 Government of India Act federates the Indian Empire.

1936: Sir James David Sifton appointed the first Governor of Bihar.

1937: Formation of[90] first Congress government in Bihar under provincial autonomy granted by British rule, Dr. Sri Krishna Sinha sworn[91] in as Chief Minister and Dr. Anugrah Narayan Sinha became[92] Deputy Chief Minister cum Finance Minister.

1942: Quit India Movement.

1946: First Cabinet of Bihar formed, consisting[79] of two members: Dr. Sri Krishna Sinha as first Chief Minister of Bihar and Dr. Anugrah Narayan Sinha[80] as Bihar's first Deputy Chief Minister cum Finance[93] Minister(also in charge of Labour, Health, Agriculture and Irrigation).Other ministers were inducted later.

1947: Indian Independence; Bihar becomes a state in the new Dominion of India. Religious violence leads to the migration of millions of Bihari Muslims to the new Pakistani states of Sindh and East Pakistan (present-day Bangladesh).

1950: The Dominion of India is replaced by a republic in 1950. Enactment of Land Reforms bill in Bihar, and abolishment of Zamindari system.

1952:Many development projects needed for the all round development of the state initiated, be it on irrigation front or on industrial front by the state government.[94] It included several river valley projects right from Koshi, Aghaur and Sakri to several other such river projects.[95]

1952-57:Bihar rated as the best administered among the states in the country.[96]

1955 The Birla Institute of Technology(BIT) is established[97] at Mesra, Ranchi.

1957-62:Second five-year plan period, Bihar government brought several heavy industries like Barauni Oil Refinery, HEC plant at Hatia, Bokaro Steel Plant, Barauni Fertiliser Plant, Barauni Thermal Power Station, Maithon Hydel Power Station, Sulphur mines at Amjhaur, Sindri Fertiliser Plant, Kargali Coal Washery, Barauni Dairy Project, etc. for the all round development of the state.[98]

1963–1967: Sri Krishna Ballabh Sahay became Chief Minister of Bihar by defeating his contestant Mahesh Prasad Sinha with support of Satyendra Narain Sinha. In his term of government, the state underwent further massive industrialisation.

1973: Indian wealth creation begins to recover; surge in all India GDP starts again.

1975–1977: Suspension of the Republican Constitution. Bihar is the centre of resistance against the Emergency. Janata Party Came to power at Centre and in Bihar; Karpoori Thakur became CM after winning chief minister-ship battle from the[99] then Janata Party President Satyendra Narayan Sinha.

1984: Indira Gandhi Assassination leads to deadly anti-Sikh Riots in northern India, including Bihar

1988-1990: Unceremonious removal of Bihar CM Bhagwat Jha Azad, Veteran[100] Leader Satyendra Narayan Singh sworn in as Chief Minister of Bihar, Lalu Prasad Yadav became Leader Of Opposition.

1990–2005: Lalu Prasad/ Rabri Devi term of Government (RJD Party). Period marks the complete collapse of the Bihar economy, massive rise in crime, and the development of mass migration to other states in Indian Union of all classes/ castes and religions.

1992: Bihar escapes severe rioting after the destruction of Babri Masjid.

2000: Bihar divided into two states by NDA central government - The northern part retains the name "Bihar", whilst southern (and more industralised region) becomes the State of Jharkhand.

2002–2004: Deadly crime wave grips Patna and Bihar

2003: First Bihari-Bhojpuri Immigrant Worker Crisis; Bihari migrants attacked in Mumbai, and hundreds killed and tens of thousands flee Assam

2005: In Feb, Lalu Prasad/ Rabri Devi lose power after 15 years, Presidents rule declared after no party wins overall majority in lower house

2005: In November, Janta Dal (United) with the BJP wins the state election with a working majority. Nitish Kumar becomes the first NDA Chief Minister of Bihar.

2005–2007: Nitish Kumar is declared the best Chief Minister in India by the India Today magazine

2007: First Global Meet for a "Resurgent Bihar" was organised in Patna.President APJ Abdul Kalam inaugurated the meet.Bhojpuri cinema hall complex bombed in Punjab. 6 UP and Bihari migrant workers killed.

2008: Second Bihari-Bhojpuri Immigrant Worker Crisis: Migrants killed in racially motivated hate attacks in Maharashtra, Assam, Manipur, and Nagaland. Hundreads of thousands flee back to Bihar and UP's Purvanchal territory. Bihar economy makes remarkable recovery in Q1 2008, resulting in labour shortages in Punjab, Maharashtra.[101]

Bihar

From Wikipedia, the free encyclopedia

Jump to navigationJump to search

For other uses, see Bihar (disambiguation).

This article may require copy editing for grammar, style, cohesion, tone, or spelling. You can assist by editing it. (August 2019) (Learn how and when to remove this template message)

Bihar

State

Clockwise from top: Great Buddha Statue at Bodh Gaya, Ruins of ancient Nalanda University, Madhubani painting from Mithila region, Brahma Kund hot springs in Rajgir

Emblem

Location of Bihar in India

Coordinates (Patna): 25.4°N 85.1°ECoordinates: 25.4°N 85.1°E

Country India

Formation22 March 1912

(Bihar Diwas)

Statehood26 January 1950

CapitalPatna

Largest cityPatna

Districts38

Government

- GovernorPhagu Chauhan (BJP)[1]
- Chief MinisterNitish Kumar (JD(U))
- Deputy Chief MinisterSushil Kumar Modi[2] (BJP)
- LegislatureBicameral

Legislative Council 75

Legislative Assembly 243

- High CourtPatna High Court

Area

[3]

- Total94,163 km2 (36,357 sq mi)

Area rank12[th]

Population

(2011)[4]

- Total103,804,637
- Rank3[rd]
- Density1,102/km2 (2,850/sq mi)
- Major Ethnolinguistic GroupsBhojpuris, Maithils, Magahis

Demonym(s)Bihari

GDP (2017–18)

[5]

- Total?4.88 lakh crore (US$68 billion)
- Per capita?38,860 (US$540)

Languages

- OfficialHindi[6]
- Additional officialMaithilia,[7] Urdub [8]

Time zoneUTC+05:30 (IST)

UN/LOCODEINBR

ISO 3166 codeIN-BR

Vehicle registrationBR

HDI (2017) 0.566[9] (medium) · 29th

Literacy (2011)63.82%[10]

Sex ratio (2011)918 ♀/1000 ♂[11]

Websitegov.bih.nic.in

a. Recognized under the Eighth Schedule of the Constitution of India.

b. In 15 districts.

Bihar (/bɪˈhɑːr/; Hindi pronunciation: [bɪˈɦaːr] (listen)) is a state in eastern India. It is the twelfth-largest Indian state, with an area of 94,163 km2 (36,357 sq mi). The third-largest state by population, it is contiguous with Uttar Pradesh to its west, Nepal to the north, the northern part of West Bengal to the east, and with Jharkhand to the south. The Bihar plain is split by the river Ganges, which flows from west to east.[12] Three main regions converge in the state: Magadh, Mithila, and Bhojpur.[13]

On 15 November 2000, southern Bihar was ceded to form the new state of Jharkhand.[14] Only 11.3% of the population of Bihar lives in urban areas, which is the lowest in India after Himachal Pradesh.[15] Additionally, almost 58% of Biharis are below the age of 25, giving Bihar the highest proportion of young people of any Indian state.[16]

In ancient and classical India, the area that is now Bihar was considered a centre of power, learning, and culture.[17] From Magadha arose India's first empire, the Maurya empire, as well as one of the world's most widely adhered-to religions: Buddhism.[18] Magadha empires, notably under the Maurya and Gupta dynasties, unified large parts of South Asia under a central rule.[19] Another region of Bihar is Mithila which was an early centre of learning and the centre of the Videha kingdom.[20][21]

Since the late 1970s, Bihar has lagged far behind other Indian states in terms of social and economic development.[22][23][24] Many economists and social scientists claim that this is a direct result of the policies of the central government, such as the freight equalization policy,[25][26] its apathy towards Bihar,[16][27][28] lack of Bihari sub-nationalism,[26][29][30] and the Permanent Settlement of 1793 by the British East India Company.[26] The state government has, however, made significant strides in developing the state.[31] Improved governance has led to an economic revival in the state through increased investment in infrastructure,[32] better health care facilities, greater emphasis on education, and a reduction in crime and corruption.[33][34]

Contents

1Etymology

2History

2.1Ancient period

2.2Medieval period

2.3Colonial Era

2.4Pre- and post-Independence

3Geography and climate

4Flora and fauna

5Demographics

6Government and administration

6.1Politics

7Public Health

8Economy

8.1Agriculture

8.2Industry

8.3Income distribution

9Culture

9.1Language and literature

9.2Paintings

9.3Performing arts

9.4Cinema

10Religion

11Media

12Transport

12.1Airways

12.2Inland Waterways

13Tourism

14Education

15See also

16References

17Further reading

18External links

Etymology

The name Bihar is derived from the Sanskrit and Pali word vihāra (Devanagari: विहार), meaning "abode". The region roughly encompassing the present state was dotted with Buddhist viharas, the abodes of Buddhist monks in the ancient and medieval periods. Medieval writer Minhaj al-Siraj Juzjani records in the Tabaqat-i Nasiri that in 1198 Bakhtiyar Khalji committed a massacre in a town identified with the word, later known as Bihar Sharif, about 70 km away from Bodh Gaya.[35][36]

History

Main article: History of Bihar

See also: Timeline for Bihar; Magadha; Mithila Kingdom; History of Buddhism in India; Decline of Buddhism in India; Mithila, India; and List of rulers of Mithila

Ancient period

Copy of the seal excavated from Kundpur, Vaishali. The Brahmi letters on the seal state: "Kundpur was in Vaishali. Prince Vardhaman (Mahavira) used this seal after the Judgement."

Magadha, Anga and Vajjian Confederacy of Mithila in circa 600 BCE.

Chirand, on the northern bank of the Ganga River, in Saran district, has an archaeological record from the Neolithic age (about 2500–1345 BC).[37][38] Regions of Bihar—such as Magadha, Mithila and Anga—are mentioned in religious texts and epics of ancient India.

Mithila gained prominence after the establishment of the Videha Kingdom[39][40] in ancient India. During the late Vedic period (c. 1100-500 BCE), Videha became one of the major political and cultural centers of South Asia, along with Kuru and Pañcāla. The kings of the Videha Kingdom were called Janakas.[41] Sita, a daughter of one of the Janaks of Mithila is mentioned as the consort of Lord Rama, in the Hindu epic, Ramayana, written by Valmiki.[39][42][page needed] The Videha Kingdom later became incorporated into the Vajji confederacy which had its capital in the city of Vaishali, which is also in Mithila.[43] Vajji had a republican form of government where the king was elected from the number of rajas. Based on the information found in texts pertaining to Jainism and Buddhism, Vajji was established as a republic by the 6th century BCE, before the birth of Gautama Buddha in 563 BCE, making it the first known republic in India.

The Haryanka dynasty, founded in 684 BC, ruled Magadha from the city of Rajgriha (modern Rajgir). The two well-known kings from this dynasty were Bimbisara and his son Ajatashatru, who imprisoned his father to ascend the throne. Ajatashatru founded the city of Pataliputra which later became the capital of Magadha. He declared war and conquered the Vajji. The Haryanka dynasty was followed by the Shishunaga dynasty. Later the Nanda Dynasty ruled a vast tract stretching from Bengal to Punjab.

The Nanda dynasty was replaced by the Maurya Empire, India's first empire. The Maurya Empire and the religion of Buddhism arose in the region that now makes up modern Bihar. The Mauryan Empire, which originated from Magadha in 325 BC, was founded by Chandragupta Maurya, who was born in Magadha. It had its capital at Pataliputra (modern Patna). The Mauryan emperor, Ashoka, who was born in Pataliputra (Patna) is believed to be one of the greatest rulers in the history of the world.[44][45]

The Gupta Empire, which originated in Magadha in 240 AD, is referred as the Golden Age of India in science, mathematics, astronomy, commerce, religion, and Indian philosophy.[46] Bihar and Bengal was invaded by Rajendra Chola I of the Chola dynasty in the 11th century.[47][48]

Medieval period

Kalidasa's Sanskrit play Abhijñānaśākuntalam

Buddhism in Magadha went into decline due to the invasion of Muhammad bin Bakhtiyar Khalji, during which many of the viharas and the famed universities of Nalanda and Vikramashila were destroyed. It was claimed that thousands of Buddhist monks were massacred during the 12th century.[49][50][51] D. N. Jha suggests, instead, that these incidents were the result of Buddhist-Brahmin skirmishes in a fight for supremacy.[52] After the fall of the Pala Empire, the Chero dynasty ruled some parts of Bihar from the 12th century to the 16th century until Mughal rule.[53] In 1540, the great Pathan chieftain, Sher Shah Suri, from Sasaram, took northern India from the Mughals, defeating the Mughal army of Emperor Humayun. Sher Shah declared Delhi his capital.

From the 11th century to the 20th century, Mithila was ruled by various indigenous dynasties. The first of these were the Karnatas, followed by the Oiniwar dynasty and finally Raj Darbhanga.[54] It was during this period that the capital of Mithila was shifted to Darbhanga.[55][56]

The tenth and the last Guru of Sikhism, Guru Gobind Singh was born in Patna.

With political instability in Mughal Empire following Aurangzeb's death, Murshid Quli Khan declared Bengal independent and himself Nawab of Bengal.

Colonial Era

After the Battle of Buxar (1764), the British East India Company obtained the diwani rights (rights to administer, and collect revenue or tax) for Bihar, Bengal and Odisha. The rich resources of fertile land, water and skilled labour had attracted the foreign imperialists, particularly the Dutch and British, in the 18th century. A number of agriculture-based industries had been started in Bihar by foreign entrepreneurs.[57] Bihar remained a part of the Bengal Presidency of British India until 1912, when the province of Bihar and Orissa was carved out as a separate province.

Pre- and post-Independence

(Sitting L to R): Rajendra Prasad and Anugrah Narayan Sinha during Mahatma Gandhi's 1917 Champaran Satyagraha

Farmers in Champaran had revolted against indigo cultivation in 1914 (at Pipra) and 1916 (Turkaulia). In April 1917, Mahatma Gandhi visited Champaran, where Raj Kumar Shukla had drawn his attention to the exploitation of the peasants by European indigo planters. The Champaran Satyagraha that followed received support from many Bihari nationalists, such as Rajendra Prasad and Anugrah Narayan Sinha.[58][59]

In the northern and central regions of Bihar, the Kisan Sabha (peasant movement) was an important consequence of the independence movement. It began in 1929 under the leadership of Swami Sahajanand Saraswati who formed the Bihar Provincial Kisan Sabha (BPKS), to mobilise peasant grievances against the zamindari attacks on their occupancy rights. The movement intensified and spread from Bihar across the rest of India, culminating in the formation of the All India Kisan Sabha (AIKS) at the Lucknow session of the Indian National Congress in April 1936, where Saraswati was elected as its first president.[60]

Bihari migrant workers have faced violence and prejudice in many parts of India, such as Maharashtra, Punjab and Assam after independence.[61][62]

See also: 2008 attacks on North Indians in Maharashtra

Geography and climate

Main articles: Geography of Bihar and Climate of Bihar

River Map of Bihar

Mountain of Ashrams, near Sena Village, at Buddha Gaya

Flooded farmlands in northern Bihar during the 2008 Bihar flood

Climate

ClassificationCwa

Avg. temperature27 °C (81 °F)

• Summer34 °C (93 °F)

• Winter10 °C (50 °F)

Precipitation1,200 mm (47 in)

Bihar has a diverse climate. Its temperature is subtropical in general, with hot summers and cold winters. Bihar is a vast stretch of fertile plain. It is drained by the Ganges River, including its northern tributaries Gandak and Koshi, originating in the Nepal Himalayas and the Bagmati originating in the Kathmandu Valley that regularly flood parts of the Bihar plains. The total area covered by the state of Bihar is 94,163 km2 (36,357 sq mi). the state is located between 24°-20'-10" N ~ 27°-31'-15" N latitude and between 83°-19'-50" E ~ 88°-17'-40" E longitude. Its average elevation above sea level is 173 feet (53 m).

The Ganges divides Bihar into two unequal halves and flows through the middle from west to east. Other Ganges tributaries are the Son, Budhi Gandak, Chandan, Orhani and Phalgu. Though the Himalayas begin at the foothills, a short distance inside Nepal and to the north of Bihar, the mountains influence Bihar's landforms, climate, hydrology and culture. Central parts of Bihar have some small hills, for example, the Rajgir hills. To the south is the Chota Nagpur plateau, which was part of Bihar until 2000 but now is part of a separate state called Jharkhand.

Flora and fauna

Bauhinia acuminata, locally known as Kachnaar

Main articles: Flora of Bihar and Fauna of Bihar

See also: Protected areas of Bihar

Bihar has notified forest area of 6,845 km2 (2,643 sq mi), which is 7.27% of its geographical area.[63] The sub Himalayan foothill of Someshwar and the Dun ranges in the Champaran district are another belt of moist deciduous forests. These also consist of shrubs, grass and reeds. Here the rainfall is above 1,600 millimetres (63 in) and thus promotes luxuriant Sal forests in the area. The most important trees are Shorea Robusta, Sal Cedrela Toona, Khair, and Semal. Deciduous forests also occur in the Saharsa and Purnia districts.[64] Shorea robusta (sal), Diospyros melanoxylon (kendu), Boswellia serrata (salai), Terminalia tomentose (asan), Terminalia bellerica (bahera), Terminalia Arjuna (arjun), Pterocarpus marsupium (paisar), Madhuca indica (mahua) are the common flora across the forest of Bihar.

Valmiki National Park, West Champaran district, covering about 800 km2 (309 sq mi) of forest, is the 18th Tiger Reserve of India and is ranked fourth in terms of density of tiger population.[65] It has a diverse landscape, sheltering rich wildlife habitats and floral and faunal composition, along with the prime protected carnivores. Vikramshila Gangetic Dolphin Sanctuary in Bhagalpur region is a sanctuary of the endangered Gangetic dolphin.[63]

Karkatgarh Waterfall on Karmanasa River is a natural habitat of crocodiles. In 2016, the government of Bihar has accepted the proposal of the forest authorities to turn the place into a Crocodile Conservation Reserve (CCR).[66]

Other notable sanctuaries include Kaimur Wildlife Sanctuary, Bhimbandh Wildlife Sanctuary and Gautam Buddha Wildlife Sanctuary.

Other species include leopard, bear, hyena, bison, chital and barking deer. Crocodiles (including muggers) and Gangetic turtles can be found in the river systems. Many varieties of local bird species as well as migratory birds can be seen in natural wetlands of Kanwar Lake Bird Sanctuary, Baraila lake, Kusheshwar Nath Lake, Udaypur lake. Nagi Dam and Nakti Dam have been declared as bird sanctuary.[63]

Demographics

Main article: Demographics of Bihar

See also: Bihari people and List of cities in Bihar by population

showPopulation growth

Languages of Bihar (2011)[68]

  Hindi (77.52%)

  Maithili (12.55%)

  Urdu (8.42%)

  Bengali (0.78%)

  Santali (0.44%)

  Other (0.29%)

After the 2011 Census, Bihar was the third most populous state of India with total population of 104,099,452 (54,278,157 male and 49,821,295 female). Nearly 89% of Bihar's population lived in rural areas. The density was 1,106. The sex ratio was 918 females per 1000 males.[69] Almost 58% of Bihar's population was below 25 years age, which is the highest in India. Most of Bihar's population belongs to Indo-Aryan-speaking ethnic groups along with few Dravidian-speaking and Austroasiatic-speaking people mostly in Chhotanagpur Plateau (now part of Jharkhand). It also attracted Punjabi Hindu refugees during the Partition of British India in 1947.[70] Bihar has a total literacy rate of 63.82% (73.39% for males and 53.33% for females), recording a growth of 20% in female literacy over the period of a decade.[10]

At 11.3%, Bihar has the second lowest urbanisation rate in India.[71] As of the 2011 census, population density surpassed 1,000 per square kilometre, making Bihar India's most densely-populated state, but still lower than West Java or Banten of Indonesia.

According to the 2011 census, 82.7% of Bihar's population practised Hinduism, while 16.9% followed Islam.[72][73]

Government and administration

Main articles: Government of Bihar and Administration in Bihar

See also: Divisions of Bihar and Districts of Bihar

Vidhansabha Building, Patna

The constitutional head of the government of Bihar is the governor, who is appointed by the President of India. The real executive power rests with the chief minister and the cabinet. The political party or the coalition of political parties having a majority in the Legislative Assembly forms the government.

The head of the bureaucracy of the state is the chief secretary. Under this position, is a hierarchy of officials drawn from the Indian Administrative Service, Indian Police Service, Indian Forest Service, and different wings of the state civil services. The judiciary is headed by the Chief Justice. Bihar has a High Court which has been functioning since 1916. All the branches of the government are located in the state capital, Patna.

The state is divided into nine divisions and 38 districts, for administrative purposes. Bihar has 12 Municipal Corporations, 49 Nagar Parishads, and 80 Nagar Panchayats.[74][75][76][77][78]

Politics

Main article: Politics of Bihar

See also: Political parties in Bihar, Elections in Bihar and List of politicians from Bihar; 2015 Bihar Legislative Assembly election

By 2004, 14 years after Lalu Prasad Yadav's victory, The Economist magazine said that "Bihar [had] become a byword for the worst of India, of widespread and inescapable poverty, of corrupt politicians indistinguishable from mafia-dons they patronise, caste-ridden social order that has retained the worst feudal cruelties".[79] In 2005, the World Bank believed that issues faced by the state were "enormous" because of "persistent poverty, complex social stratification, unsatisfactory infrastructure and weak governance".[80] Currently, there are two main political formations: the National Democratic Alliance (NDA) which comprises Bharatiya Janata Party, Lok Janashakti Party, Rashtriya Lok Samta Party, Hindustani Awam Morcha and JD(U) (Joined recently after breaking the Grand Alliance with RJD and INC), Second is alliance between RJD and Indian National Congress. There are many other political formations. The Communist Party of India had a strong presence in Bihar at one time, but is weakened now.[81] The CPM and Forward Bloc have a minor presence, along with the other extreme Left.[82]

In contrast to prior governments, which emphasized divisions of caste and religion, Nitish Kumar's manifesto was based on economic development, curbs on crime and corruption and greater social equality for all sections of society. Since 2010, the government has confiscated the properties of corrupt officials and redeployed them as schools buildings.[83] Simultaneously they introduced Bihar Special Court Act to curb crime.[84] It has also legislated for a two-hour break on Fridays, including lunch, to enable Muslim employees to pray and thus cut down on post-lunch absenteeism by them.[85] The government has prohibited the sale and consumption of alcohol in the state since March 2016;[86] this ban has been linked to a drop in tourism to Bihar[87] and rise in substance abuse.[88]

Public Health

In Bihar, attempts have been made to establish a well-functioning department of public health. National efforts like the National Health Mission, the Clinical Establishments Act of 2010, and the formation of the Empowered Action Group (EAG)[89] catalyze the disbursement of federal funds by expanding healthcare access and improving the quality of healthcare services to states in need. However, Bihar's ability to fully utilize this funding is lacking. Bihar's health care system has the appropriate policies in place to allow for the implementation of comprehensive healthcare treatment. However, it is in the execution and management of the funding and services where it falls behind. Overall, the lack of consistent monitoring tools for policy evaluation explain why a strategic, evidence based public health system has been slow to take root in the state of Bihar. Consequently, Bihar generally ranks weakest in health outcomes in comparison to other Indian states and even among its EAG counterparts.[90][91]

Research indicates that Bihar relies on privatized hospitals to provide healthcare to the masses, it has high levels of unacknowledged corruption and also implements a vertical system of disease management. In fact, the ratio of private spending on health care relative to public spending in Bihar is the second highest in India.[90] These factors have been found to be associated with slower healthcare delivery and a higher degree of economic burden as a consequence of steep healthcare costs.[92][93][94][95] Much of this is because Bihar lacks in the continuity and transparency of health reporting as required by the Clinical Establishments Act of 2010. In turn, this prevents the government from making evidence based conclusions about policy changes and hospital effectiveness. Rather,

Bihar's health department displays patterns of ill-informed spending, inconsistent hiring, and erratic spending on healthcare infrastructure.

For example, according to the Government of India's "Ministry of Health & Family Welfare Health and Family Welfare Census Data 2008-2015",[96] the number of healthcare professionals including registered nurses, auxiliary nurses, physicians and health supervisors at each hospital in Bihar have remained significantly lower compared to those working in Kerala, and do not seem to follow any sort of pattern. Rather, its number of registered healthcare professionals remains constant over time. Compared to Bihar, we see that Kerala's number of registered healthcare professionals consistently increase over time. According to "Rural Health Statistics 2015", the greatest shortfalls exist among physicians and specialists across the state at least 75%.[90] This extends to the number of actual health centers across Bihar as well, as it only has 50% of the sub-health centers, 60% of the primary health centers, and a mere 9% of the community health centers it needs based on the national government's supply to population norms. At a closer look, the number of hospital beds that Bihar includes in each government-run hospital actually decreased between 2008 and 2015, compared to the consistently increasing number of hospital beds in government-run Kerala hospitals.[96] Given the population of Bihar (population: 99 million) is much denser than Kerala (population: 35 million), these numbers suggest that Bihar is significantly behind in the number of healthcare professionals that should be employed within the state.[97][96] It is likely that because there is a lack of data reporting, analysis and evaluation within Bihar that these trends exist.

Despite these shortcomings, Bihar has shown gradual signs of public health improvement in a few areas. There is indeed a shortage of skilled healthcare professionals, but Bihar still benefits from a surplus of female health workers compared to male health workers.[90] In terms of key impact indicators, between 2010 and 2013, the crude birth rate decreased by 2.3%, crude death rate decreased by 5.6%, infant mortality rate decreased by 12.7%, neo-natal mortality rate decreased by 8.6%, under 5 mortality rate decreased by 9.1%, and maternal mortality ratio decreased by 10.2%.[90]

It would suit Bihar well to continue to adapt common cost effective practices to strengthen their health systems data measurement and research.[91] Research has shown that the implementation of patient and caregiver surveys, exit interviews at health centers, vignettes, and audit studies are simple methods of bolstering reporting and evaluation in lower income areas such as Bihar.[98]

Economy

Main article: Economy of Bihar

YearGross State Domestic Product
(millions of Indian Rupees)[99]

1980

73,530

1985

142,950

1990

264,290

1995

244,830

2000

469,430

2005

710,060

[100]2010

2,042,890

[citation needed]2015

3,694,690

[citation needed]

Bihar accounts for 71% of India's annual litchi production.[101]

A village market

Gross state domestic product of Bihar for the year 2013/2014 has been around 3683.37 billion INR. By sectors, its composition is:

Agriculture = 22%

Industry = 5%

Services = 73%.

Bihar is the fastest growing state in terms of gross state domestic product (GSDP), clocking a growth rate of 17.06% in FY 2014–15.[102] The economy of Bihar was projected to grow at a compound annual growth rate (CAGR) of 13.4% during 2012–2017, i.e. the 12th Five-Year Plan. Bihar has witnessed strong growth in per capita net state domestic product (NSDP). At current prices, per capita NSDP of the state grew at a CAGR of 12.91 per cent during 2004–05 to 2014–15.[103] Bihar's per capita income went up by 40.6 per cent in the financial year 2014–15.[104]

Agriculture

Bihar is the fourth-largest producer of vegetables and the eighth-largest producer of fruits in India. Bihar has high agricultural production making it one of the strongest sectors of the state. About 80 percent of the state's population is employed in agriculture, which is higher as compared to India's average.[103] The main agricultural products produced in Bihar are litchi, guava, mango, pineapple, brinjal, lady's finger, cauliflower, cabbage, rice, wheat and sugarcane, and sunflower. Though good soil and favourable climatic conditions such as good rainfall favour agriculture, it has to encounter flood threat as well, which may drain off the fertile soil, if not conserved properly.[105] The state (mostly southern parts) faces droughts almost every year affecting production of crops such as paddy.[106]

Industry

Prior to prohibition, Bihar emerged as a brewery hub with major domestic and foreign firms setting up production units in the state.[107] In August 2018, United Breweries Limited announced it would begin production of non-alcoholic beer at its previously defunct brewery in Bihar.[108][109]

Hajipur, Dalmianagar and Barauni are the major industrial city in Bihar[110]

The state's debt was estimated at 77% of GDP by 2007.[111] The Finance Ministry has given top priority to create investment opportunities for big industrial houses like Reliance Industries. Further developments have taken place in the growth of small industries, improvements in IT infrastructure, the new software park in Patna, Darbhanga, Bhagalpur[112] and the completion of the expressway from the Purvanchal border through Bihar to Jharkhand. In August 2008, a Patna registered company called the Security and Intelligence Services[113] took over the Australian guard and mobile patrol services business of American conglomerate, United Technologies Corporation (UTC). SIS is registered and taxed in Bihar.[114] The capital city, Patna, is one of the better-off cities in India when measured by per capita income.[115]^ The State Government is setting up an Information Technology (IT) City at Rajgir in Nalanda district.[116] Additionally, India's first Media Hub is also proposed to be set up in Bihar.[117]

Income distribution

In terms of income, the districts of Patna, Munger, and Begusarai were the three best-off out of a total of 38 districts in the state, recording the highest per capita gross district domestic product of ?31,441, ?10,087 and ?9,312, respectively, in 2004–05.[115]

Culture

Main article: Culture of Bihar

Paag of Mithila

Language and literature

Main articles: Languages in Bihar and Literature in Bihar

See also: Maithili language, Bhojpuri, Angika, Magahi, Magadhi Prakrit, Hindi in Bihar, and Urdu Language in Bihar

Maithili language in Tirhuta and Devanagari scripts

Hindi is the official language of the state.[6] Urdu is the second official language in 15 districts of the state.[8] Maithili (including its dialect Bajjika), Bhojpuri, Angika and Magahi are also widely spoken in the state.[118][119] Maithili is a recognised regional language of India under the Eighth Schedule to the Constitution of India.[7] Proponents are calling for Bhojpuri and Magahi to receive the same status.[120]

Paintings

See also: Mithila painting

Mithila Painting is also known as Madhubani art is a distinct type of painting style hailing from Mithila region of Bihar

There are several traditional styles of painting practiced in Bihar. One is Mithila painting, a style of Indian painting used in the Mithila region of Bihar. Traditionally, the painting was one of the skills that was passed down from generation to generation in the families of the Mithila region, mainly by women. Painting was usually done on walls during festivals, religious events, and other milestones of the life cycle, like birth, Upanayanam (the sacred thread ceremony), and marriage.[121]

Mithila painting was traditionally done on huts' freshly plastered mud walls, but today it is also done on cloth, handmade paper, and canvas. Famous Mithila painters have included Smt Bharti Dayal, Mahasundari Devi, the late Ganga Devi, and Sita Devi.

Mithila painting is also called Madhubani art. It mostly depicts human beings and their association with nature. Common scenes illustrate deities like Krishna, Ram, Shiva, Durga Lakshmi, and Saraswati from ancient epics. Natural objects like the sun, moon, and religious plants like Tulsi are also widely painted, along with scenes from the royal court and social events like weddings. Generally, no space is left empty.[121]

Historically, the Patna School of Painting (Patna Salaam), sometimes called Company Painting, flourished in Bihar during the early 18th to mid-20th centuries. The Patna School of Painting was an offshoot of the well-known Mughal Miniature School of Painting. Those who practiced this art form were descendants of Hindu artisans of Mughal painting. Facing persecution from the Mughal Emperor, Aurangzeb, these artisans found refuge, via Murshidabad, in Patna during the late 18th century. Their art shared the characteristics of the Mughal painters, but whereas the Mughal style depicted only royalty and court scenes, the Patna artists also started painting bazaar scenes. They used watercolours on paper and on mica. The style's subject matter evolved to include scenes of Indian daily life, local rulers, festivals, and ceremonies. This school of painting formed the basis for the formation of the Patna Art School under the leadership of Shri Radha Mohan. The school is an important center of the fine arts in Bihar.

Performing arts

See also: Music of Bihar

Bihar has produced musicians like Bharat Ratna Ustad Bismillah Khan and dhrupad singers like the Malliks (Darbhanga Gharana) and the Mishras (Bettiah Gharana) along with poets like Vidyapati Thakur who contributed to Maithili Music. The classical music in Bihar is a form of the Hindustani classical music. Gaya is another centre of excellence in classical music, particularly of the Tappa and Thumri varieties. Pandit Govardhan Mishra – son of the Ram Prasad Mishra, himself an accomplished singer – is perhaps the finest living exponent of Tappa singing in India today, according to Padma Shri Gajendra Narayan Singh, founding secretary of the Sangeet Natak Academi of Bihar. Gajendra Narayan Singh also writes, in his memoir, that Champanagar, Banaili, was another major centre of classical music. Rajkumar Shyamanand Sinha of Champanagar, Banaili princely state, was a great patron of music and was himself one of the finest exponents of classical vocal music in Bihar in his time.[122] Singh, in another book on Indian classical music, has written that "Kumar Shyamanand Singh of Banaili estate had such expertise in singing that many great singers including Kesarbai Kerkar acknowledged his ability. After listening to bandishes from Kumar Sahib, Pandit Jasraj was moved to tears and lamented that, alas, he did not have such ability himself." [free translation of Hindi text].[123][124]

During the 19th century, when the condition of Bihar worsened under the British misrule, many Biharis had to emigrate as indentured labourers to the West Indies, Fiji, and Mauritius. During this time many sad plays and songs called birha became popular, in the Bhojpur region, thus Bhojpuri Birha. Dramas incorporating this theme continue to be popular in the theatres of Patna.[125][better source needed]

Vidyapati

Magahi folk singers

Bharat Ratna Ustad Bismillah Khan, from Dumraon, Bihar.

Cinema

Main article: Cinema of Bihar

See also: Bhojpuri Film Industry and List of Bhojpuri films

Anurita Jha acted as the lead actress in Maithili film Mithila Makhaan

Bihar has a robust Bhojpuri-language film industry. There is also a smaller production of Magadhi-, Maithili-, as well as Angika-language films. The first film with Bhojpuri dialogue was Ganga Jamuna, released in 1961.[126] Bhaiyaa, the first Magadhi film, was released in 1961.[127] The first Maithili movie was Kanyadan released in 1965.[128] Maithili film Mithila Makhaan won the National Film Award for Best Maithili Film in 2016.[129] The history of films entirely in Bhojpuri begins in 1962 with the well-received film Ganga Maiyya Tohe Piyari Chadhaibo ("Mother Ganges, I will offer you a yellow sari"), which was directed by Kundan Kumar.[130] 1963's Lagi nahin chute ram was the all-time hit Bhojpuri film, and had higher attendance than Mughal-e-Azam in the eastern and northern regions of India. Bollywood's Nadiya Ke Paar is another of the most famous Bhojpuri-language movies. However, in the following years, films were produced only in fits and starts. Films such as Bidesiya ("Foreigner", 1963, directed by S. N. Tripathi) and Ganga ("Ganges", 1965, directed by Kundan Kumar) were profitable and popular, but in general Bhojpuri films were not commonly produced in the 1960s and 1970s.

In the 1980s, enough Bhojpuri films were produced to tentatively support a dedicated industry. Films such as Mai ("Mom", 1989, directed by Rajkumar Sharma) and Hamar Bhauji ("My Brother's Wife", 1983, directed by Kalpataru) continued to have at least sporadic success at the box office. However, this trend faded out by the end of the decade, and by 1990, the nascent industry seemed to be completely finished.[131]

The Bhojpuri film industry took off again in 2001 with the super hit Saiyyan Hamar ("My Sweetheart", directed by Mohan Prasad), which vaulted the hero of that film, Ravi Kishan, to superstardom.[132] This success was quickly followed by several other remarkably successful films, including Panditji Batai Na Biyah Kab Hoi ("Priest, tell me when I will marry", 2005, directed by Mohan Prasad) and Sasura Bada Paisa Wala ("My father-in-law, the rich guy", 2005). In a measure of the Bhojpuri film industry's rise, both of these did much better business in the states of Uttar Pradesh and Bihar than mainstream Bollywood hits at the time, and both films, made on extremely tight budgets, earned back more than ten times their production costs.[133] Sasura Bada Paisa Wala also introduced Manoj Tiwari, formerly a well-loved folk singer, to the wider audiences of Bhojpuri cinema. The success of Ravi Kishan and Manoj Tiwari's films has led to a dramatic increase in Bhojpuri cinema's visibility, and the industry now supports an awards show[134] and a trade magazine, Bhojpuri City,[135] which chronicles the production and release of what are now over one hundred films per year.

Religion

Main article: Religion in Bihar

<div style="border:solid transparent;position:absolute;width:100px;line-height:0;<div style="border:solid transparent;position:absolute;width:100px;line-height:0;

Religions in Bihar (2011)[72]

Hinduism (82.69%)

Islam (16.87%)

Christianity (0.12%)

Other religions (0.31%)

Hindu Goddess Sita, the consort of Lord Rama is believed to be born in Sitamarhi district in the Mithila region of modern-day Bihar.[136][137] Gautama Buddha attained Enlightenment at Bodh Gaya, a town located in the modern day district of Gaya in Bihar. Vasupujya, the 12th Jain Tirthankara was born in Champapuri, Bhagalpur. Vardhamana Mahavira, the 24th and the last Tirthankara of Jainism, was born in Vaishali around the 6th century BC.[138]

Portrait of Goddess Sita

Vishnupadh Temple, Gaya, Bihar

Buddha's statue at Bodh Gaya's temple

31 feet Statue of Lord Vasupujya, Champapur, Bhagalpur

Sita Kund at Sitamarhi, Mithila, Bihar is believed to be the birthplace of Hindu Goddess Sita[139]

Buddha's Statue - Bihar Museum

Media

Main article: Media in Bihar

Biharbandhu was the first Hindi newspaper published in Bihar. It was started in 1872 by Madan Mohan Bhatta, a Marathi Brahman who settled in Bihar Sharif.[140] Hindi journalism in Bihar, and specially Patna, could make little headway initially. Many Hindi journals were born and, after a lapse of time, vanished. Many journals were shelved even in the planning stages.[141] But once Hindi had the support of being an official language, it started making inroads, even into the remote areas of Bihar. Hindi journalism acquired wisdom and maturity, and its longevity was assured. Hindi was introduced in the law courts in Bihar in 1880.[140][142]

Urdu journalism and poetry has a glorious past in Bihar. Many poets belong to Bihar, such as Shaad Azimabadi, Kaif Azimabadi, and Kalim Ajiz. Shanurahman, a world-famous radio announcer, is from Bihar. Many Urdu dailies—such as Qomi Tanzim and Sahara—are published in Bihar. There is a monthly Urdu magazine called Voice of Bihar – which is the first of its kind and is becoming popular among the Urdu speaking people.

The beginning of the 20th century was marked by a number of notable new publications. A monthly magazine named Bharat Ratna was started in Patna, in 1901. It was followed by Ksahtriya Hitaishi, Aryavarta from Dinapure, Udyoga, and Chaitanya Chandrika.[143] Udyog was edited by Vijyaanand Tripathy, a famous poet of the time, and Chaitanya Chandrika by Krishna Chaitanya Goswami, a literary figure of that time. The literary activity was not confined to Patna alone but to other districts of Bihar.[140][144]

Hindustan, Dainik Jagran, Rajasthan Patrika, Aaj, and Prabhat Khabar are some of the Hindi newspapers of Bihar. National English dailies like The Times of India, Hindustan Times, Navbharat Times, The Telegraph, and The Economic Times have readers in the urban regions.

Transport

Main article: Transport in Bihar

Patna river port on national inland waterways-1 at Gai Ghat

Steamers and dredgers at Gai Ghat, Patna

Airways

Bihar has two operational airports: Lok Nayak Jayaprakash Airport, Patna; and Gaya Airport.

Inland Waterways

The Ganges – navigable throughout the year – was the principal river highway across the vast north Indo-Gangetic Plain. Vessels capable of accommodating five hundred merchants were known to ply this river in the ancient period; it served as a conduit for overseas trade, as goods were carried from Pataliputra (later Patna) and Champa (later Bhagalpur) out to the seas and to ports in Sri Lanka and Southeast Asia. The role of the Ganges as a channel for trade was enhanced by its natural links – it embraces all the major rivers and streams in both north and south Bihar.[145]

Tourism

Main article: Tourism in Bihar

The Mahabodhi Temple, among the four holy sites related to the life of the Lord Buddha and UNESCO World Heritage Site

The culture and heritage of Bihar can be observed from the large number of ancient monuments spread throughout the state. Bihar is visited by many tourists from around the world,[146] with about 24,000,000 (24 million) tourists visiting the state each year.[146]

In earlier days, tourism in the region was purely based on educational tourism, as Bihar was home of some prominent ancient universities like Nalanda and Vikramashila.[147][148]

Sabhyata Dwar in Patna
Monuments of Darbhanga
Remains of the ancient city of Vaishali
Trolley ride in Rajgir
The tomb of Sher Shah Suri is in the Sasaram town of Bihar
Barabar Caves – Asokan Inscription
Vikramshila Monastery
Buddha Smriti Park
Education
Main articles: Education in Bihar and Literacy in Bihar
See also: List of educational institutions in Bihar
Front view of administrative building of IIT Patna

Historically, Bihar has been a major centre of learning, home to the ancient universities of Nalanda (established in 450 CE), Odantapurā (established in 550CE) and Vikramashila (established in 783 CE).[149] This tradition of learning may have been stultified during the period of Turkic invasions, c. 1000 CE, at which point it is believed major education centers, maintained by reclusive communities of Buddhist monks removed from the local populace, were suppressed by the Turkic raids originating from central Asia .[150]

Bihar saw a revival of its education system during the later part of the British rule, when Patna University, the seventh oldest university of the Indian subcontinent, was established in 1917.[151] Some other centres of high learning established under British rule are Patna College (established 1839), Bihar School of Engineering (1900; now known as National Institute of Technology, Patna), Prince of Wales Medical College (1925; now Patna Medical College and Hospital), Science College, Patna (1928), Patna Women's College, Bihar Veterinary College (established 1927), Imperial Agriculture Research Institute (1905; now Dr. Rajendra Prasad Central Agriculture University, Pusa) among others.

A recent survey by Pratham rated the receptivity of Bihari children to their teaching as being better than those in other states.[152] Bihar is striving to increase female literacy, now at 53.3%, as the government establishes educational institutions. At the time of independence, women's literacy in Bihar was 4.22%.

Literacy rate from 1951 to 2011[153]
YearTotalMalesFemales
196121.9535.858.11
197123.1735.869.86
198132.3247.1116.61
199137.4951.3721.99
200147.5360.3233.57
201163.8273.3953.33

In 1964 Bihar School of Yoga was established at Munger.

Bihar has a National Institute of Technology (NIT) and an Indian Institute of Technology (IIT) in Patna. The National Employability Report of Engineering Graduates, 2014[154] puts graduates from Bihar in the top 25 percent of the country, and rating Bihar as one of the three top states at producing engineering graduates in terms of quality and employability.[155]

As of December 2013, there are seven government engineering colleges in the public sector, and 12 engineering colleges in the private sector, in Bihar, besides government-aided BIT Patna and Women's Institute of Technology, Darbhanga. The overall annual intake of students of these technical institutes in Bihar is only 6,200.[156][157][158]

In Bihar, government colleges are located at Muzaffarpur, Bhagalpur, Gaya, Darbhanga, Motihari, Nalanda, and Saran (Chhapra). All institutes are recognised by All India Council for Technical Education (AICTE), affiliated with Aryabhatta Knowledge University (AKU). As it is, the foundation stone of the eighth engineering college of the state government, Ramdhari Singh Dinkar Engineering College, was laid on 22 December 2013 at Begusarai,[159][160] while the process of creating the infrastructure for two new engineering colleges – one each at Madhepura and Sitamarhi – has started.[161][162]

NIT Patna main building

NIT Patna is the second oldest engineering college of India. Its origin can be traced to 1886, with the establishment of a survey training school, subsequently renamed Bihar College of Engineering in 1932. In 2004, the government of India upgraded the college to National Institute of Technology (NIT) status. In 2007, NIT Patna was granted Institute of National Importance status, in accordance with the National Institutes of Technology Act, 2007.

Bihar established several new educational institutes between 2006 and 2008. BIT Mesra started its Patna extension centre in September 2006. On 8 August 2008, Indian Institutes of Technology Patna was inaugurated with students from all over India[163] In 2008, NSIT opened its new college in Bihta, which is now emerging as an education hub.[164][165] BCE, Bhagalpur, MIT, Muzaffarpur, and the National Institute of Pharmaceutical Education and Research, Hajipur (NIPER)[166] are in Bihar. On 4 August 2008, National Institute of Fashion Technology Patna was established as the ninth such institute in India.[167] Chanakya National Law University and Chandragupt Institute of Management were established in the later half of 2008. Steps are being taken to revive the ancient Nalanda Mahavihara as Nalanda International University. Countries such as Japan, Korea, and China have also taken initiatives. The A.N. Sinha Institute[168] of Social Studies is a premier research institute in the state.

Bihar e-Governance Services & Technologies (BeST) and the government of Bihar have initiated a unique program to establish a centre of excellence called Bihar Knowledge Center, a finishing school to equip students with the latest skills and customised short-term training programs at an affordable cost. The centre aims to attract the youth of the state to improve their technical, professional, and soft skills, to meet the current requirements of the industrial job market.[169]

Bihar has the Central Institute of Plastic Engineering & Technology (CIPET) and the Institute of Hotel Management (a central government unit) in Hajipur. The Central University of Bihar (CUB) is one of the sixteen central universities newly established by the Government of India under the Central Universities Act, 2009 (Section 25 of 2009). The university is temporarily located on the premises of the Birla Institute of Technology, Patna. The university is likely to be relocated to Panchanpur, approximately 10 kilometres (6.2 mi) from Gaya, on 300 acres (120 ha) of land to be transferred soon from the military. On 28 February 2014, Lok Sabha Speaker Meira Kumar laid the foundation stone.

In 2010 Government of Bihar established Bihar Agricultural University at Sabour in Bhagalpur district. It has ten colleges. Mahatma Gandhi Central University—also established under the Central Universities Act, and Amendment Act of 2014—is situated in Motihari, the district headquarters of East Champaran district. The All India Institute of Medical Sciences, Patna was established in 2012. On 3 July 2013, chief minister Nitish Kumar laid foundation stone for a new campus of National Institute of Electronics & Information Technology in Amara cillage, near Bihta township.[170] It was inaugurated in February 2018.[171] Bihar has eight medical colleges which are funded by the government, namely Patna Medical College and Hospital, Nalanda Medical College and Hospital, Vardhman Institute of Medical Sciences, Indira Gandhi Institute of Medical Sciences, Darbhanga Medical College and Hospital, Anugrah Narayan Magadh Medical College and Hospital Gaya, Sri Krishna Medical College and Hospital, Jawaharlal Nehru Medical College, Bhagalpur, Government Medical College, Bettiah and five private medical colleges[172]

In February 2019, deputy chief minister Sushil Modi announced the Bihar government's planned to establish 11 new medical colleges at Chhapra, Purnia, Samastipur, Bengusarai, Sitamarhi, Vaishali, Jhanjharpur, Siwan, Buxar, Bhojpur, Jamui and a dental college at Rahui in Nalanda district is under construction. There are also plans on constructing a cancer institute within Indira Gandhi Institute of Medical Sciences premises and transformation of Patna Medical College and Hospital into a world-class health centre.[173] In 2014 the government of Bihar established Development Management Institute in Bihta near the Patna.Nalanda University was re-established in 2014. In 2015, the central government had proposed re-establishment of Vikramshila in Bhagalpur and had designated ? 500crores for it.[174] The Indian Institute of Management Bodh Gaya was established in 2015. In 2016 the government of Bihar established Patliputra University, Munger University, Purnea University through Bihar state university bill. The government of Bihar established Bihar Animal Science University in 2017. It has three constituent colleges namely, Bihar Veterinary College, Sanjay Gandhi Institute of Dairy Technology (Patna) and College of Fisheries, Kishanganj.[175] The Indian Institute of Information Technology, Bhagalpur, was established in 2017. In March 2019, the government of Bihar has sent a proposal to centre Government to upgrade Darbhanga Medical College and Hospital into an AIIMS-like institution.[176]

West Bengal

"Paschim Banga" redirects here. For other uses, see Paschimbanga.

West Bengal

Paschim Banga

State

From top: Kolkata Skyline from Howrah,
Dakshineswar Kali Temple near Kolkata, Kolkata Gate, also known as the Biswa Bangla Gate at New Town, Tea garden in the Dooars region, Hazarduari Palace in Murshidabad, Sunrise in Digha beach, Bengal tiger in Sundarbans National Park,
View of Darjeeling from Happy Valley Tea Estate

Emblem

Location of West Bengal in India

Country India

Established26 January 1950

CapitalKolkata

Largest city

KolkataDistricts

List[show]

Government

• BodyGovernment of West Bengal

• GovernorJagdeep Dhankhar (BJP)[1]

• Chief MinisterMamata Banerjee (AITC)

• LegislatureLegislative Assembly (295)

• High CourtCalcutta High Court

• Chief JusticeThottathil B. Radhakrishnan

Area

• Total88,752 km2 (34,267 sq mi)

Area rank13th

Population

(2011)[2]

• Total91,347,736

• Rank4th

• Density1,029/km2 (2,670/sq mi)

Demonym(s)Bengali

GDP (2018–19)

[3][4]

• Total?11.77 lakh crore (US$170 billion)

• Per capita?116,831 (US$1,600)

Languages

• Official

Bengali

English[5]

- Additional officialNepali in two sub-divisions of Darjeeling[6]

Urdu

Hindi

Odia

Santali

Punjabi

Kamtapuri

Rajbanshi

Kurmali[7][8][9]

in blocks, subdivisions or districts exceeding 10% of the population

Time zoneUTC+05:30 (IST)

ISO 3166 codeIN-WB

Vehicle registrationWB

HDI (2017) 0.637 (medium) · 21st[10]

Literacy (2011)77.08%[11]

Sex ratio (2011)950 ♀/1000 ♂[12]

WebsiteOfficial website

^* 294 elected, 1 nominated

West Bengal (/bɛnˈɡɔːl/; Bengali: Paschim Banga) is a state in the eastern region of India along the Bay of Bengal. With over 91 million inhabitants (as of 2011), it is India's fourth-most populous state. West Bengal is the thirteenth-largest Indian state, with an area of 88,752 km2 (34,267 sq mi). Part of the ethno-linguistic Bengal region of the Indian subcontinent, it borders Bangladesh in the east, and Nepal and Bhutan in the north. It also borders the Indian states of Odisha, Jharkhand, Bihar, Sikkim, and Assam. The state capital is Kolkata (Calcutta) the seventh-largest city in India, and center of the third-largest metropolitan area in the country. West Bengal includes the Darjeeling Himalayan hill region, the Ganges delta, the Rarh region, and the coastal Sundarbans. The main ethnic group is the Bengalis, with Bengali Hindus forming the demographic majority.

The area's early history featured a succession of Indian empires, internal squabbling, and a tussle between Hinduism and Buddhism for dominance. Ancient Bengal was the site of several major Janapadas (kingdoms), while the earliest cities date back to the Vedic period. The region was part of several ancient pan–Indian empires, including the Mauryans and Guptas. It was also a bastion of regional kingdoms. The citadel of Gauda served as the capital of the Gauda Kingdom, the Buddhist Pala Empire (8th–11th century) and Hindu Sena Empire (11th–12th century). Islam was introduced through trade with the Abbasid Caliphate, but following the early conquest of Muhammad bin Bakhtiyar Khalji and the establishment of the Delhi Sultanate, it spread across the entire Bengal region. Later, occasional Muslim raiders reinforced the process of conversion by building mosques, madrasas, and khanqahs. During the Islamic Bengal Sultanate, founded in 1352, Bengal was a major trading nation in the world and was often referred by the Europeans as the richest country to trade with. It was absorbed into the Mughal Empire in 1576. Simultaneously, some parts of the region were ruled by several Hindu states, and Baro-Bhuyan landlords, and part of it was briefly overrun by the Suri Empire. The Mughal Bengal was heralded by Aurangzeb as the "paradise of the nations",[13] since it was the empire's most economically developed province. It became a leading exporter to the world,[14][15][16] and a center of worldwide industries such as cotton textiles, silk,[17] and shipbuilding.[18] Its citizens' standard of living was among the world's highest.[19][20] Bengal accounted for 40% of Dutch imports from Asia, for example, including more than 50% of its textiles and around 80% of its silks.[14] Bengal's economy bypassed the period of proto-industrialization.[21]

By the 18th century, the state was ruled by the Nawabs of Bengal, before being conquered by the British East India Company at the Battle of Plassey in 1757.[22][23] Calcutta served for many years as the capital of British India. The region was later administered by the United Kingdom as part of the Bengal Presidency (1757–1905; 1912–1947) and Eastern Bengal and Assam Province (1905–1912) in British India.[24][25] Bengal faced multiple famines and deindustrialisation under British Raj.[26][27] The socio-cultural movements of the Bengal

Renaissance played an influential role in decolonisation and the region was a hotbed of the Indian independence movement.[28] In 1947, the Bengal Legislative Council and the Bengal Legislative Assembly voted on the Partition of Bengal along religious lines into two separate entities: West Bengal, a state of India, and East Bengal, a province of Pakistan which later became the independent Bangladesh. Several regional and pan–Indian empires throughout Bengal's history have shaped its culture, cuisine, and architecture.

Post independence, West Bengal's economy is based on agricultural production and small and medium-sized enterprises.[29] The economy of West Bengal is the sixth-largest state economy in India with ?11.77 lakh crore (US$170 billion) in gross domestic product and a per capita GDP of ?116,000 (US$1,600).[3][4] The state has high government debt with ?3.6 lakh crore (US$50 billion) or 35% of GSDP, moderate unemployment, and low per capita income.[30][31] In human development index it ranks twenty-first among Indian states.[10] Kolkata is known as the "cultural capital of India".[32] West Bengal has two World Heritage sites and one of the top tourism destinations in India.[33][34]

Contents

Etymology

Main article: Names of Bengal

The origin of the name Bengal (Bangla and Bongo in Bengali) is unknown. One theory suggests the word derives from "Bang", the name of a Dravidian tribe that settled the region around 1000 BCE.[35] The Bengali word Bongo might have been derived from the ancient kingdom of Vanga (or Banga). Although some early Sanskrit literature mentions the name Vanga, the region's early history is obscure.[36]

In 1947, at the end of British rule over the Indian subcontinent the Bengal Legislative Council and the Bengal Legislative Assembly voted on the Partition of Bengal along religious lines into two separate entities: West Bengal, which continued as an Indian state, and East Bengal, a province of Pakistan, which came to be known be as East Pakistan and later became the independent Bangladesh.[37][38]

In 2011 the Government of West Bengal proposed a change in the official name of the state to PaschimBanga (Bengali: পশ্চিমবঙ্গ Pôshchimbônggô).[39] This is the native name of the state, literally meaning "western Bengal" in the native Bengali language. In August 2016 the West Bengal Legislative Assembly passed another resolution to change the name of West Bengal to "Bengal" in English, and "Bangla" in Bengali. Despite the Trinamool Congress government's efforts to forge a consensus on the name change resolution, the Indian National Congress, the Left Front, and the Bharatiya Janata Party opposed the resolution.[40] However, the central government has turned down the proposal maintaining the state should have one single name for all languages instead of three, and it should not be the same as that of any other territory (pointing out that the name 'Bangla' may create confusion with neighbouring Bangladesh).[40][41][42]

History

Main articles: History of Bengal and History of West Bengal

Ancient and classical period

Coin of the King Shashanka, who created the first separate political entity in Bengal, called the Gauda Kingdom.

Stone Age tools dating back 20,000 years have been excavated in the state, showing human occupation 8,000 years earlier than scholars had thought.[43] According to the Indian epic Mahabharata the region was part of the Vanga Kingdom.[44] Several Vedic realms were present in the Bengal region, including Vanga, Rarh, Pundravardhana, and the Suhma Kingdom. One of the earliest foreign references to Bengal is a mention by the Ancient Greeks around 100 BCE of a land named Gangaridai located at the mouths of the Ganges.[45] Bengal had overseas trade relations with Suvarnabhumi (Burma, Lower Thailand, the Lower Malay Peninsula, and Sumatra).[46] According to the Sri Lankan chronicle Mahavamsa, Prince Vijaya (c. 543 – c. 505 BCE), a Vanga Kingdom prince, conquered Lanka (modern-day Sri Lanka) and named the country Sinhala Kingdom.[47]

The kingdom of Magadha was formed in the 7th century BCE, consisting of the regions now comprising Bihar and Bengal. It was one of the four main kingdoms of India at the time of the lives of Mahavira, the principal figure of Jainism, and Gautama Buddha, founder of Buddhism. It consisted of several janapadas, or kingdoms.[48] Under Ashoka, the Maurya Empire of Magadha in the 3rd century BCE extended over nearly all of South Asia, including Afghanistan and parts of Balochistan. From the 3rd to the 6th centuries CE, the kingdom of Magadha served as the seat of the Gupta Empire.[49]

The Pala Empire was an imperial power during the Late Classical period on the Indian subcontinent, which originated in the region of Bengal.

Two kingdoms—Vanga or Samatata, and Gauda—are said in some texts to have appeared after the end of the Gupta Empire although details of their ascendancy are uncertain.[50] The first recorded independent king of Bengal was Shashanka, who reigned in the early 7th century.[51] Shashanka is often recorded in Buddhist annals as an intolerant Hindu ruler noted for his persecution of the Buddhists. He murdered Rajyavardhana, the Buddhist king of Thanesar, and is noted for destroying the Bodhi tree at Bodhgaya, and replacing Buddha statues with Shiva lingams.[52] After a period of anarchy,[53]:36 the Pala dynasty ruled the region for four hundred years beginning in the 8th century. A shorter reign of the Hindu Sena dynasty followed.[54]

Rajendra Chola I of the Chola dynasty invaded some areas of Bengal between 1021 and 1023.[55]

Islam was introduced through trade with the Abbasid Caliphate.[56] Following the early conquest of Muhammad bin Bakhtiyar Khalji and the establishment of the Delhi Sultanate, it spread across the entire Bengal region. Later, occasional Muslim raiders reinforced the process of conversion by building mosques, madrasas, and khanqahs. During the Islamic Bengal Sultanate, founded in 1352, Bengal was major world trading nation and was often referred by the Europeans as the richest country with which to trade.[57] Later, in 1576, it was absorbed into the Mughal Empire.[58]

Medieval and early modern periods

Firoz Minar at Gauḍa was built during the Bengal Sultanate.

Subsequent Muslim conquests helped spread Islam throughout the region.[59] It was ruled by dynasties of the Bengal Sultanate and feudal lords under the Delhi Sultanate for the next few hundred years. The Bengal Sultanate was interrupted for twenty years by a Hindu uprising under Raja Ganesha. In the 16ᵗʰ century, Mughal general Islam Khan conquered Bengal. Administration by governors appointed by the court of the Mughal Empire gave way to semi-independence under the Nawabs of Murshidabad, who nominally respected the sovereignty of the Mughals in Delhi. Several independent Hindu states were established in Bengal during the Mughal period, including those of Pratapaditya of Jessore District and Raja Sitaram Ray of Bardhaman. The Koch dynasty in northern Bengal flourished during the 16ᵗʰ and 17ᵗʰ centuries; it weathered the Mughals and survived until the advent of the British colonial era.[60][61]

Colonial period

An 1880 map of Bengal

Several European traders reached this area in the late 15ᵗʰ century. The British East India Company defeated Siraj ud-Daulah, the last independent Nawab, in the Battle of Plassey in 1757. The company gained the right to collect revenue in Bengal subah (province) in 1765 with the signing of the treaty between the East India company and the Mughal emperor following the Battle of Buxar in 1764.[62] The Bengal Presidency was established in 1765; it later incorporated all British-controlled territory north of the Central Provinces (now Madhya Pradesh), from the mouths of the Ganges and the Brahmaputra to the Himalayas and the Punjab. The Bengal famine of 1770 claimed millions of lives due to tax policies enacted by the British company.[63] Calcutta, the headquarters of the East India company, was named the capital of British-held territories in India in 1773.[64] The failed Indian rebellion of 1857 started near Calcutta and resulted in a transfer of authority to the British Crown,[65] administered by the Viceroy of India.[66]

The Bengal Renaissance and the Brahmo Samaj socio-cultural reform movements significantly influenced the cultural and economic life of Bengal.[67] Between 1905 and 1911 an abortive attempt was made to divide the province of Bengal into two zones.[68] Bengal suffered from the Great Bengal famine in 1943, which claimed three million lives during World War II.[69] Bengalis played a major role in the Indian independence movement, in which revolutionary groups such as Anushilan Samiti and Jugantar were dominant. Armed attempts against the British Raj from Bengal reached a climax when news of Subhas Chandra Bose leading the Indian National Army against the British reached Bengal. The Indian National Army was subsequently routed by the British.[70]

Indian independence and afterwards

When India gained independence in 1947, Bengal was partitioned along religious lines. The western part went to the Dominion of India and was named West Bengal. The eastern part went to the Dominion of Pakistan as a province called East Bengal (later renamed East Pakistan in 1956), becoming the independent nation of Bangladesh in 1971.[71] In 1950 the Princely State of Cooch Behar merged with West Bengal.[72] In 1955 the former French enclave of Chandannagar, which had passed into Indian control after 1950, was integrated into West Bengal; portions of Bihar were also subsequently merged with West Bengal. Both West and East Bengal experienced large influxes of refugees during and after partition in 1947. Refugee resettlement and related issues continued to play a significant role in the politics and socio-economic condition of the state.[72]

The Darjeeling Himalayan Railway was designated a UNESCO World Heritage Site in 1999.

During the 1970s and 1980s, severe power shortages, strikes, and a violent Naxalite movement damaged much of the state's infrastructure, leading to a period of economic stagnation. The Bangladesh Liberation War of 1971 resulted in an influx of millions of refugees to West Bengal, causing significant strains on its infrastructure.[73] The 1974 smallpox epidemic killed thousands. West Bengal politics underwent a major change when the Left Front won the 1977 assembly election, defeating the incumbent Indian National Congress. The Left Front, led by the Communist Party of India (Marxist), governed the state for the next three decades.[74]

The state's economic recovery gathered momentum after the central government introduced economic liberalisations in the mid-1990s. This was aided by the advent of information technology and IT-enabled services. Beginning in the mid-2000s, armed activists conducted minor terrorist attacks in some parts of the state.[75][76] Clashes with the administration took place at several controversial locations over the issue of industrial land acquisition.[77][78] This became a decisive reason behind the defeat of the ruling Left Front government in the 2011 assembly election.[79] Although the economy was severely damaged during the unrest in the 1970s, the state has managed to revive its economy steadily throughout the years.[80][81][82] The state has shown improvement regarding bandhs (strikes)[83][84][85] and educational infrastructure.[86] Significant strides have been made in reducing unemployment,[87] though the state suffers from substandard healthcare services,[88][89] a lack of socio-economic development,[90] poor infrastructure,[91][92] unemployment, and civil violence.[93][94] In 2006 the state's healthcare system was severely criticised in the aftermath of the West Bengal blood test kit scam.[95][96]

Geography and climate

Main articles: Geography of West Bengal and Climate of West Bengal

Many areas remain flooded during the heavy rains brought by a monsoon.

West Bengal is on the eastern bottleneck of India, stretching from the Himalayas in the north to the Bay of Bengal in the south. The state has a total area of 88,752 square kilometres (34,267 sq mi).[2] The Darjeeling Himalayan hill region in the northern extreme of the state is a part of the eastern Himalayas mountain range. In this region is Sandakfu, which, at 3,636 m (11,929 ft), is the highest peak in the state.[97] The narrow Terai region separates the hills from the North Bengal plains, which in turn transitions into the Ganges delta towards the south. The Rarh region intervenes between the Ganges delta in the east and the western plateau and high lands. A small coastal region is in the extreme south, while the Sundarbans mangrove forests form a geographical landmark at the Ganges delta.[98]

The main river in West Bengal is the Ganges, which divides into two branches. One branch enters Bangladesh as the Padma, or Pôdda, while the other flows through West Bengal as the Bhagirathi River and Hooghly River. The Farakka barrage over the Ganges feeds the Hooghly branch of the river by a feeder canal. Its water flow management has been a source of lingering dispute between India and Bangladesh.[99] The Teesta, Torsa, Jaldhaka, and Mahananda rivers are in the northern hilly region. The western plateau region has rivers like the Damodar, Ajay, and Kangsabati. The Ganges delta and the Sundarbans area have numerous rivers and creeks. Pollution of the Ganges from indiscriminate waste dumped into the river is a major problem.[100] Damodar, another tributary of the Ganges and once known as the "Sorrow of Bengal" (due to its frequent floods), has several dams under the Damodar Valley Project. At least nine districts in the state suffer from arsenic contamination of groundwater, and as of 2017 an estimated 1.04 crore people were afflicted by arsenic poisoning.[101]

West Bengal's climate varies from tropical savanna in the southern portions to humid subtropical in the north. The main seasons are summer, the rainy season, a short autumn, and winter. While the summer in the delta region is noted for excessive humidity, the western highlands experience a dry summer like northern India. The highest daytime temperatures range from 38 °C (100 °F) to 45 °C (113 °F).[102] At night, a cool southerly breeze carries moisture from the Bay of Bengal. In early summer, brief squalls and thunderstorms known as Kalbaisakhi, or Nor'westers, often occur.[103] West Bengal receives the Bay of Bengal branch of the Indian Ocean monsoon that moves in a southeast to northwest direction. Monsoons bring rain to the whole state from June to September. Heavy rainfall of above 250 centimetres (98 in) is observed in the Darjeeling, Jalpaiguri, and Cooch Behar district. During the arrival of the monsoons, low pressure in the Bay of Bengal region often leads to the formation of storms in the coastal areas. Winter (December–January) is mild over the plains with average minimum temperatures of 15 °C (59 °F).[102] A cold and dry northern wind blows in the winter, substantially lowering the humidity level. The Darjeeling Himalayan Hill region experiences a harsh winter, with occasional snowfall.[104]

Flora and fauna

A Bengal tiger

Sal trees in the Arabari forest in West Midnapur

The "India State of Forest Report 2017", recorded forest area in the state is 16,847 km2 (6,505 sq mi),[105][106] while in 2013, forest area was 16,805 km2 (6,488 sq mi), which was 18.93% of the state's geographical area, compared to the then national average of 21.23%.[107] Reserves and protected and unclassed forests constitute 59.4%, 31.8%, and 8.9%, respectively, of forested areas, as of 2009.[108] Part of the world's largest mangrove forest, the Sundarbans in southern West Bengal.[109]

West Bengal State Symbols

TitleSymbolImage

State animalFishing cat[110]

State birdWhite-throated kingfisher

State flowerNight-flowering jasmine[110]

State treeDevil tree[110]

From a phytogeographic viewpoint, the southern part of West Bengal can be divided into two regions: the Gangetic plain and the littoral mangrove forests of the Sundarbans.[111] The alluvial soil of the Gangetic plain, combined with favourable rainfall, makes this region especially fertile.[111] Much of the vegetation of the western part of the state has similar species composition with the plants of the Chota Nagpur plateau in the adjoining state of Jharkhand.[111] The predominant commercial tree species is Shorea robusta, commonly known as the sal tree. The coastal region of Purba Medinipur exhibits coastal vegetation; the predominant tree is the Casuarina. A notable tree from the Sundarbans is the ubiquitous sundari (Heritiera fomes), from which the forest gets its name.[112]

The distribution of vegetation in northern West Bengal is dictated by elevation and precipitation. For example, the foothills of the Himalayas, the Dooars, are densely wooded with sal and other tropical evergreen trees.[113] Above an elevation of 1,000 metres (3,300 ft), the forest becomes predominantly subtropical. In Darjeeling, which is above 1,500 metres (4,900 ft), temperate forest trees like oaks, conifers, and rhododendrons predominate.[113]

3.26% of the geographical area of West Bengal is protected land, comprising fifteen wildlife sanctuaries and five national parks—Sundarbans National Park, Buxa Tiger Reserve, Gorumara National Park, Neora Valley National Park, and Singalila National Park.[108] Extant wildlife includes Indian rhinoceros, Indian elephant, deer, leopard, gaur, tiger, and crocodiles, as well as many bird species. Migratory birds come to the state during the winter.[114] The high-altitude forests of Singalila National Park shelter barking deer, red panda, chinkara, takin, serow, pangolin, minivet, and kalij pheasants. The Sundarbans are noted for a reserve project devoted to conserving the endangered Bengal tiger, although the forest hosts many other endangered species such as the Gangetic dolphin, river terrapin, and estuarine crocodile.[115] The mangrove forest also acts as a natural fish nursery, supporting coastal fishes along the Bay of Bengal.[115] Recognising its special conservation value, the Sundarbans area has been declared a Biosphere Reserve.[108]

Government and politics

Main articles: Government of West Bengal and Politics of West Bengal

See also: Council of Ministers of West Bengal and List of Chief Ministers of West Bengal

West Bengal is governed through a parliamentary system of representative democracy, a feature the state shares with other Indian states. Universal suffrage is granted to residents. There are two branches of government. The legislature, the West Bengal Legislative Assembly, consists of elected members and special office bearers such as the Speaker and Deputy Speaker, who are elected by the members. Assembly meetings are presided over by the Speaker or the Deputy Speaker in the Speaker's absence. The judiciary is composed of the Calcutta High Court and a system of lower courts. Executive authority is vested in the Council of Ministers headed by the Chief Minister although the titular head of government is the Governor. The Governor is the Head of State appointed by the President of India. The leader of the party or coalition with a majority in the Legislative Assembly is appointed as the Chief Minister by the Governor. The Council of Ministers are appointed by the Governor on the advice of the Chief Minister. The Council of Ministers reports to the Legislative Assembly. The Assembly is unicameral with 295 members, or MLAs,[116] including one nominated from the Anglo-Indian community. Terms of office run for five years, unless the Assembly is dissolved prior to the completion of the term. Auxiliary authorities known as panchayats, for which local body elections are regularly held, govern local affairs. The state contributes 42 seats to the Lok Sabha[117] and 16 seats to the Rajya Sabha of the Indian Parliament.[118]

Main offices in West Bengal

Raj Bhavan, the residence of the governor of the state

West Bengal Legislative Assembly

Calcutta High Court, highest court in West Bengal

Nabanna, office of Chief Minister of West Bengal

Writers' Building, West Bengal Government Secretariat

The main players in the politics of the state are the All India Trinamool Congress, Bharatiya Janata Party, Congress, and the Left Front alliance (led by the Communist Party of India (Marxist) or CPI(M)). Following the West Bengal State Assembly Election in 2011, the All India Trinamool Congress and Indian National Congress coalition under Mamata Banerjee of the All India Trinamool Congress was elected to power with 225 seats in the legislature.[119] Prior to this, West Bengal was ruled by the Left Front for 34 years (1977–2011), making it the world's longest-running democratically elected communist government.[74] Banerjee was re-elected as Chief Minister in the 2016 election in which Trinamool Congress won an absolute majority.[120]

The state has one autonomous region, the Gorkhaland Territorial Administration.[121]

Districts

Main article: List of districts of West Bengal

Districts of West Bengal

A hut in a village in the Hooghly district

As of 2017, West Bengal is divided into 23 districts.[122]

DistrictPopulationGrowth rateSex ratioLiteracyDensity per square Kilometer

North 24 Parganas10,009,78112.0495584.062445

South 24 Parganas8,161,96118.1795677.51819

Purba Bardhaman4,835,432−94574.73890

Paschim Bardhaman2,882,031−92278.751800

Murshidabad7,103,80721.0995866.591334

West Midnapore5,913,45713.8696678.00631

Hooghly5,519,1459.4696181.801753

Nadia5,167,60012.2294774.971316

East Midnapore5,095,87515.3693887.021081

Howrah4,850,02913.5093983.313306

Kolkata4,496,69−1.6790886.3124306

Maldah3,988,84521.2294461.731069

Jalpaiguri3,872,84613.8795373.25622

Alipurduar[a]1,700,000−−−400

Bankura3,596,29212.6495470.95523

Birbhum3,502,40416.1595670.68771

North Dinajpur3,007,13423.1593959.07958

Purulia2,930,11515.5295764.48468

Cooch Behar2,819,08613.7194274.78832

Darjeeling1,846,82314.7797079.56586

Dakshin Dinajpur1,676,27611.5295672.82755

Kalimpong[a]202,239−−−270

Jhargram[a]1,136,548−−−374

^ Jump up to:a b c Was created after the 2011 Census

Each district is governed by a district collector or district magistrate, appointed by either the Indian Administrative Service or the West Bengal Civil Service.[123] Each district is subdivided into sub-divisions, governed by a Sub-Divisional Magistrate, and again into blocks. Blocks consists of panchayats (village councils) and town municipalities.[124]

The capital and largest city of the state is Kolkata—the third-largest urban agglomeration[125] and the seventh-largest city[126] in India. Asansol is the second-largest city and urban agglomeration in West Bengal.[125] Siliguri is an economically important city, strategically located in the northeastern Siliguri Corridor (Chicken's Neck) of

India.[127] Other larger cities and towns in West Bengal are: Durgapur, Howrah, Bardhaman, Baharampur, Jalpaiguri, Kharagpur, and Chandannagar.[128]

Economy

Main article: Economy of West Bengal

Net State Domestic Product at Factor Cost at Current Prices (2004–05 Base)[129]

(figures in crores of Indian rupees)

YearNet State Domestic Product

2004–2005190,073

2005–2006209,642

2006–2007238,625

2007–2008272,166

2008–2009309,799

2009–2010366,318

The Grand Hotel in Kolkata. Tourism, especially from Bangladesh, is an important part of West Bengal's economy.

As of 2015, West Bengal has the sixth-highest GSDP in India. GSDP at current prices (base 2004–2005) has increased from Rs 2,086.56 billion in 2004–05 to Rs 8,00,868 crores in 2014–2015,[130] reaching Rs 10,21,000 crores in 2017–18.[131] GSDP percent growth at current prices varied from a low of 10.3% in 2010–2011 to a high of 17.11% in 2013–2014. The growth rate was 13.35% in 2014–2015.[132] The state's per capita income has lagged the all India average for over two decades. As of 2014–2015, per capita NSDP at current prices was Rs 78,903.[132] Per-capita NSDP growth rate at current prices varied from 9.4% in 2010–2011 to a high of 16.15% in 2013–2014. The growth rate was 12.62% in 2014–2015.[133]

In 2015–2016, percentage share of Gross Value Added (GVA) at factor cost by economic activity at constant price (base year 2011–2012) was Agriculture-Forestry and Fishery—4.84%, Industry 18.51% and Services 66.65%. It has been observed that there has been a slow but steady decline in the percentage share of industry and agriculture over the years.[134] Agriculture is the leading economic sector in West Bengal. Rice is the state's principal food crop. Rice, potato, jute, sugarcane, and wheat are the state's top five crops.[135]:14 Tea is produced commercially in northern districts; the region is well known for Darjeeling and other high-quality teas.[135]:14 State industries are localised in the Kolkata region, the mineral-rich western highlands, and the Haldia Port region.[136] The Durgapur-Asansol colliery belt is home to a number of steel plants.[136] Important manufacturing industries include: engineering products, electronics, electrical equipment, cables, steel, leather, textiles, jewellery, frigates, automobiles, railway coaches, and wagons. The Durgapur centre has established a number of industries in the areas of tea, sugar, chemicals, and fertilisers. Natural resources like tea and jute in nearby areas has made West Bengal a major centre for the jute and tea industries.[137]

Years after independence, West Bengal is dependent on the central government for help in meeting its demands for food; food production remained stagnant, and the Indian green revolution bypassed the state. However, there has been a significant increase in food production since the 1980s, and the state now has a surplus of grains.[138] The state's share of total industrial output in India was 9.8% in 1980–1981, declining to 5% by 1997–1998. In contrast, the service sector has grown at a rate higher than the national rate.[138] The state's total financial debt stood at ?1,918,350 million (US$27 billion) as of 2011.[139]

Freshly sown saplings of rice in a paddy; in the background are stacks of jute sticks.

In the period 2004–2010, the average gross state domestic product (GSDP) growth rate was 13.9% (calculated in Indian rupee terms) lower than 15.5%, the average for all states of the country.[135]:4

The economy of West Bengal has witnessed many surprising changes in direction. The agricultural sector in particular rose to 8.33% in 2010–11 before tumbling to −4.01% in 2012–13.[140] Many major industries such as the Uttarpara Hindustan Motors car manufacturing unit, the jute industry, and the Haldia Petrochemicals unit experienced shutdowns in 2014. In the same year, plans for a 300 billion Jindal Steel project was mothballed. The tea industry of West Bengal has also witnessed shutdowns for financial and political reasons.[141] The tourism industry of West Bengal was negatively impacted in 2017 because of the Gorkhaland agitation.[142]

However, over the years due to effective changes in the stance towards industrialisation, ease of doing business has improved in West Bengal.[143][144][145] Steps are being taken to remedy this situation by promoting West Bengal as an investment destination. A leather complex has been built in Kolkata. Smart cities are being planned close to Kolkata, and major roadway projects are in the offing to revive the economy.[146] West Bengal has been able to attract 2% of the foreign direct investment in the last decade.[147]

Transport

See also: List of airports in West Bengal

Netaji Subhash Chandra Bose International Airport is a hub for flights to and from Bangladesh, East Asia, Nepal, Bhutan and northeast India.

Durgapur Expressway

An SBSTC bus in Karunamoyee.

Kolkata Metro, India's first metro rail system

As of 2011, the total length of surface roads in West Bengal was over 92,023 kilometres (57,180 miles);[135]:18 national highways comprise 2,578 km (1,602 mi)[148] and state highways 2,393 km (1,487 mi).[135]:18 As of 2006, the road density of the state was 103.69 kilometres per square kilometre (166.87 miles per square mile), higher than the national average of 74.7 km/km2 (120.2 mi/sq mi).[149]

As of 2011, the total railway route length was around 4,481 km (2,784 mi).[135]:20 Kolkata is the headquarters of three zones of the Indian Railways—Eastern Railway and South Eastern Railway, and the Kolkata Metro, which is the newly formed 17th zone of the Indian Railways.[150][151] The Northeast Frontier Railway (NFR) serves the northern parts of the state. The Kolkata metro is the country's first underground railway.[152] The Darjeeling Himalayan Railway, part of NFR, is a UNESCO World Heritage Site.[153]

Netaji Subhas Chandra Bose International Airport at Dum Dum, Kolkata, is the state's largest airport. Bagdogra Airport near Siliguri is a customs airport that offers international service to Bhutan and Thailand, besides regular domestic service. Kazi Nazrul Islam Airport, India's first private sector airport, serves the twin cities of Asansol-Durgapur at Andal, Bardhaman.[154][155]

Kolkata is a major river port in eastern India. The Kolkata Port Trust manages the Kolkata and the Haldia docks.[156] There is passenger service to Port Blair on the Andaman and Nicobar Islands. Cargo ship service operates to ports in India and abroad, operated by the Shipping Corporation of India. Ferries are a principal mode of transport in the southern part of the state, especially in the Sundarbans area. Kolkata is the only city in India to have trams as a mode of transport; these are operated by the Calcutta Tramways Company.[157]

Several government-owned organisations operate bus services in the state, including: the Calcutta State Transport Corporation, the North Bengal State Transport Corporation, the South Bengal State Transport Corporation, the West Bengal Surface Transport Corporation and the Calcutta Tramways Company.[158] There are also private bus companies. The railway system is a nationalised service without any private investment.[159] Hired forms of transport include metered taxis and auto rickshaws, which often ply specific routes in cities. In most of the state, cycle rickshaws and in Kolkata, hand-pulled rickshaws and electric rickshaws are used for short-distance travel.[160]

Demographics

Main article: Bengali people

Dakshineswar Kali Temple

Tipu Sultan Mosque

St Paul's Cathedral

Languages of West Bengal (2011)[161]

  Bengali (86.22%)

  Hindi (6.96%)

  Santali (2.66%)

  Urdu (1.82%)

  Nepali (1.27%)

Others (1.07%)
showPopulation Growth

According to the provisional results of the 2011 national census, West Bengal is the fourth-most-populous state in India with a population of 91,347,736 (7.55% of India's population).[2] Bengalis, consisting of Bengali Hindus, Bengali Muslims, Bengali Christians and a few Bengali Buddhists, comprise the majority of the population.[163] Marwari, Maithil and Bhojpuri speakers are scattered throughout the state; various indigenous ethnic Buddhist communities such as the Sherpas, Bhutias, Lepchas, Tamangs, Yolmos, and ethnic Tibetans can be found in the Darjeeling Himalayan hill region. Native Magahi speakers are found in Malda district.[164] Surjapuri, a language considered to be a mix of Maithili and Bengali, is spoken across northern parts of the state.[165] The Darjeeling district also has a large Nepali immigrant population, making Nepali a widely spoken language there. West Bengal is also home to indigenous tribal Adivasis such as: Santhal, Munda, Oraon, Bhumij, Lodha, Kol, and Toto tribe. There are a small number of ethnic minorities primarily in the state capital, including : Chinese, Tamils, Maharashtrians, Odias, Assamese, Malayalis, Gujaratis, Anglo-Indians, Armenians, Jews, Punjabis, and Parsis.[166] India's sole Chinatown is in eastern Kolkata.[167]

The state's official languages are Bengali and English;[6] Nepali has additional official status in the three subdivisions of Darjeeling district.[6] In 2012, the state government passed a bill granting additional official statues to Hindi, Odia, Punjabi, Santali and Urdu languages in areas were speakers exceed 10% of the population.[7][9] In 2019, another bill was passed by the government to include Kamtapuri, Kurmali and Rajbanshi as additional official languages in blocks, divisions or districts where the speakers exceed 10% of the population.[8] As of 2001, in decreasing order of number of speakers, the languages of the state are: Bengali (85.27%), Hindi (7.17%), Santali (2.80%), Urdu (2.06%), and Nepali (1.28%).[6]

Religion in West Bengal (2011)[168]

Hinduism (70.54%)

Islam (27.01%)

Christianity (0.72%)

Buddhism (0.31%)

Jainism (0.07%)

Sikhism (0.07%)

Other Religions (1.03%)

Irreligion (0.25%)

West Bengal is religiously diverse, with regional cultural and religious specificities. Although Hindus are the predominant community, the state has a large minority Muslim population. Christians, Buddhists, and others form a minuscule part of the population. As of 2011, Hinduism is the most common religion, with adherents representing 70.54% of the total population.[169] Muslims, the second-largest community as well as the largest minority group, comprise 27.01% of the total population,[170] Sikhism, Christianity, Buddhism, and other religions make up the remainder.[171] Buddhism remains a prominent religion in the Himalayan region of the Darjeeling hills; almost the entirety of West Bengal's Buddhist population is from this region.[172] The state contributes 7.8% of India's population.[173] The Hindu population of West Bengal is 64,385,546 while the Muslim population is 24,654,825, according to the 2011 census.[174] The state's 2001–2011 decennial population growth rate was 13.93%,[2] lower than the 1991–2001 growth rate of 17.8%,[2] and lower than the national rate of 17.64%.[175] The gender ratio is 947 females per 1,000 males.[175] As of 2011, West Bengal had a population density of 1,029 inhabitants per square kilometre (2,670/sq mi) making it the second-most densely populated state in India, after Bihar.[175]

The literacy rate is 77.08%, higher than the national rate of 74.04%.[176] Data from 2010–2014 showed the life expectancy in the state was 70.2 years, higher than the national value of 67.9.[177][178] The proportion of people living below the poverty line in 2013 was 19.98%, a decline from 31.8% a decade ago.[179] Scheduled castes and tribes form 28.6% and 5.8% of the population, respectively, in rural areas, and 19.9% and 1.5%, respectively, in urban areas.[138]

In September 2017, West Bengal achieved 100% electrification, after some remote villages in the Sunderbans became the last to be electrified.[180]

As of September 2017, of 125 towns and cities in Bengal, 76 have achieved open defecation free (ODF) status. All towns in the districts of: Nadia, North 24 Parganas, Hooghly, Burdwan and East Midnapore are ODF zones, with Nadia becoming the first ODF district in the state in April 2015.[181][182]

A study conducted in three districts of West Bengal found that accessing private health services to treat illness had a catastrophic impact on households. This indicates the importance of public provision of health services to mitigate against poverty and the impact of illness on poor households.[183]

The latest Sample Registration System (SRS) statistical report shows that West Bengal has the lowest fertility rate among Indian states. West Bengal's total fertility rate was 1.6, lower than Bihar's 3.4, which is the highest in the entire country. Bengal's TFR of 1.6 roughly equals that of Canada.[184]

Culture

See also: Bengalis, Culture of West Bengal, and Culture of Darjeeling

Literature

Main articles: Bengali literature and History of Bengali literature

Rabindranath Tagore is Asia's first Nobel laureate and the composer of India's national anthem.

Swami Vivekananda was a key figure in introducing Vedanta and Yoga to Europe and the US,[185] raising interfaith awareness and making Hinduism a world religion.[186]

The Bengali language boasts a rich literary heritage it shares with neighbouring Bangladesh. West Bengal has a long tradition of folk literature, evidenced by the Charyapada, a collection of Buddhist mystic songs dating back to the 10th and 11th centuries; Mangalkavya, a collection of Hindu narrative poetry composed around the 13th century; Shreekrishna Kirtana, a pastoral Vaishnava drama in verse composed by Boru Chandidas; Thakurmar Jhuli, a collection of Bengali folk and fairy tales compiled by Dakshinaranjan Mitra Majumder; and stories of Gopal Bhar, a court jester in medieval Bengal. In the 19th and 20th centuries, Bengali literature was modernised in the works of authors such as Bankim Chandra Chattopadhyay, whose works marked a departure from the traditional verse-oriented writings prevalent in that period;[187] Michael Madhusudan Dutt, a pioneer in Bengali drama who introduced the use of blank verse;[188] and Rabindranath Tagore, who reshaped Bengali literature and music. Indian art saw the introduction of Contextual Modernism in the late 19th and early 20th centuries.[189] Other notable figures include Kazi Nazrul Islam, whose compositions form the avant-garde genre of Nazrul Sangeet,[190] Sarat Chandra Chattopadhyay, whose works on contemporary social practices in Bengal are widely acclaimed,[191] and Manik Bandyopadhyay, who is considered one of the leading lights of modern Bengali fiction.[192] In modern times, Jibanananda Das has been acknowledged as "the premier poet of the post-Tagore era in India".[193] Other writers include: Bibhutibhushan Bandopadhyay, best known for his work Pather Panchali; Tarashankar Bandopadhyay, well known for his portrayal of the lower strata of society;[194] Manik Bandopadhyay, a pioneering novelist; and Ashapurna Devi, Shirshendu Mukhopadhyay, Saradindu Bandopadhyay, Buddhadeb Guha, Mahashweta Devi, Samaresh Majumdar, Sanjeev Chattopadhyay, Shakti Chattopadhyay, Buddhadeb Basu,[195] Joy Goswami, and Sunil Gangopadhyay.[196][197]

Music and dance

Main article: Music of West Bengal

Baul singers at Basanta-Utsab, Shantiniketan.

Dance with Rabindra Sangeet

A notable music tradition is the Baul music, practised by the Bauls, a sect of mystic minstrels.[198] Other folk music forms include Gombhira and Bhawaiya. Folk music in West Bengal is often accompanied by the ektara, a one-stringed instrument. Shyama Sangeet is a genre of devotional songs, praising the Hindu goddess Kali;[199] kirtan is devotional group songs dedicated to the god Krishna.[200] Like other states in northern India, West Bengal also has a heritage in North Indian classical music. Rabindrasangeet, songs composed and set to words by Rabindranath Tagore, and Nazrul geeti (by Kazi Nazrul Islam) are popular. Also prominent are Dwijendralal, Atulprasad and Rajanikanta's songs, and adhunik or modern music from films and other composers.[201] From the early 1990s, new genres of music have emerged, including what has been called Bengali Jeebonmukhi Gaan (a modern genre based on realism). Bengali dance forms draw from folk traditions, especially those of the tribal groups, as well as the broader Indian dance traditions. Chhau dance of Purulia is a rare form of masked dance.[202]

Films

Main article: Cinema of West Bengal

Satyajit Ray, a pioneer in Bengali cinema along with Ravi Sankar.

West Bengali films are shot mostly in studios in the Kolkata neighbourhood of Tollygunj; the name "Tollywood" (similar to Hollywood and Bollywood) is derived from that name. The Bengali film industry is well known for its art films, and has produced acclaimed directors like Satyajit Ray who is widely regarded as one of the greatest filmmakers of the 20th century,[203] Mrinal Sen whose films were known for their artistic depiction of social reality, Tapan Sinha who was one of the most prominent Indian film directors of his time,[204] and Ritwik Ghatak. Some contemporary directors include veterans such as: Buddhadeb Dasgupta, Tarun Majumdar, Goutam Ghose, Aparna Sen, and Rituparno Ghosh, and a newer pool of directors such as Kaushik Ganguly and Srijit Mukherji.[205][206][207]

Fine arts

Panchchura Temple in Bishnupur, one of the older examples of the terracotta arts of India.

There are significant examples of fine arts in Bengal from earlier times, including the terracotta art of Hindu temples and the Kalighat paintings. Bengal has been in the vanguard of modernism in fine arts. Abanindranath Tagore, called the father of modern Indian art, started the Bengal School of Art, one of whose goals was to promote the development of styles of art outside the European realist tradition that had been taught in art colleges under the British colonial administration. The movement had many adherents, including: Gaganendranath Tagore, Ramkinkar Baij, Jamini Roy, and Rabindranath Tagore. After Indian Independence, important groups such as the Calcutta Group and the Society of Contemporary Artists were formed in Bengal and came to dominate the art scene in India.[208][209]

Reformist heritage

The capital, Kolkata, was the workplace of several social reformers, including Raja Ram Mohan Roy, Iswar Chandra Vidyasagar, and Swami Vivekananda. Their social reforms eventually led to a cultural atmosphere that made it possible for practices like sati, dowry, and caste-based discrimination, or untouchability, to be abolished.[210] The region was also home to several religious teachers, such as Chaitanya, Ramakrishna, Prabhupada, and Paramahansa Yogananda.[210]

Cuisine

Main article: Cuisine of West Bengal

Assorted food eaten in West Bengal: Patisapta, a kind of pitha; Shorshe Ilish (Hilsha with Mustard Sauce) and Rasgullas in sugar syrup

Rice and fish are traditional favourite foods, leading to a saying in Bengali, "machhe bhate bangali", that translates as "fish and rice make a Bengali".[211] Bengal's vast repertoire of fish-based dishes includes hilsa preparations, a favourite among Bengalis. There are numerous ways of cooking fish depending on its texture, size, fat content, and bones.[212] Most of the people also consume eggs, chicken, mutton, and shrimp. Panta bhat (rice soaked overnight in water) with onion and green chili is a traditional dish consumed in rural areas.[213] Common spices found in a Bengali kitchen include cumin, ajmoda (radhuni), bay leaf, mustard, ginger, green chillies, and turmeric.[214] Sweets occupy an important place in the diet of Bengalis and at their social ceremonies. Bengalis make distinctive sweetmeats from milk products, including Rôshogolla, Chômchôm, Kalojam, and several kinds of sondesh. Pitha, a kind of sweet cake, bread, or dim sum, are specialties of the winter season. Sweets such as narkol-naru, til-naru, moa, and payesh are prepared during festivals such as Lakshmi puja.[215] Popular street foods include Aloor Chop, Beguni, Kati roll, biryani, and phuchka.[216][217]

Clothing

Jamdani Sari of Bangladesh is very popular in West Bengal.

Bengali women commonly wear the sari, often distinctly designed according to local cultural customs. In urban areas, many women and men wear western attire. Among men, western dress has greater acceptance. Particularly on cultural occasions, men also wear traditional costumes such as the panjabi with dhuti while women wear salwar kameez or sari.[218]

West Bengal produces several varieties of cotton and silk saris in the country. Handlooms are a popular way for the state's rural population to earn a living through weaving. Every district has weaving clusters, which are home to artisan communities, each specialising in specific varieties of handloom weaving. Notable handloom saris include tant, jamdani, garad, korial, baluchari, tussar, and muslin.[219]

Festivals

Main article: List of festivals of West Bengal

Durga Puja is the biggest, most popular and widely celebrated festival in West Bengal.[220] The five-day-long colourful Hindu festival includes intense celebration across the state. Pandals are erected in various cities, towns, and villages throughout West Bengal. The city of Kolkata undergoes a transformation during Durga Puja. It is decked up in lighting decorations and thousands of colourful pandals are set up where effigies of the goddess Durga and her four children are displayed and worshipped. The idols of the goddess are brought in from Kumortuli, where idol-makers work throughout the year fashioning clay-models of the goddess. Since independence in 1947, Durga Puja has slowly changed into more of a glamorous carnival than a religious festival. Today people of diverse religious and ethnic backgrounds partake in the festivities.[221] On Vijayadashami, the last day of the festival, the effigies are paraded through the streets with riotous pageantry before being dumped into the rivers.[222]

Rath Yatra is a Hindu festival which celebrates Jagannath, a form of Krishna. It is celebrated with much fanfare in Kolkata as well as in rural Bengal. Images of Jagannath are set upon a chariot and pulled through the streets.[223]

Festivals of West Bengal: Durga Puja, Rath Yatra and Muharram procession in Kolkata.

Other major festivals of West Bengal include: Poila Baishakh the Bengali new year, Dolyatra or Holi the festival of lights, Poush Parbon, Kali Puja, Nabadwip Shakta Rash, Saraswati Puja, Deepaboli, Lakshmi Puja, Janmashtami, Jagaddhatri Puja, Vishwakarma Puja, Bhai Phonta, Rakhi Bandhan, Kalpataru Day, Shivratri, Ganesh Chathurthi, Maghotsav, Kartik Puja, Akshay Tritiya, Raas Yatra, Guru Purnima, Annapurna Puja, Charak Puja, Gajan, Buddha Purnima, Christmas, Eid ul-Fitr, Eid ul-Adha, and Muharram. Rabindra Jayanti, Kolkata Book Fair, Kolkata Film Festival, and Nazrul Jayanti. All are important cultural events.[223]

Eid al-Fitr is the most important Muslim festival in West Bengal. They celebrate the end of Ramadan with prayers, alms-giving, shopping, gift-giving, and feasting.[224]

Christmas, called Bôṛodin (Great day) is perhaps the next major festival celebrated in Kolkata, after Durga Puja. Just like Durga Puja, Christmas in Kolkata is an occasion when all communities and people of every religion take part. The state tourism department organises a gala Christmas Festival every year in Park Street.[225] The whole of Park Street is hung with colourful lights, and food stalls sell cakes, chocolates, Chinese cuisine, momo, and various other items. The state invites musical groups from Darjeeling and other North East India states to perform choir recitals, carols, and jazz numbers.[226] Buddha Purnima, which marks the birth of Gautama Buddha, is one of the most important Hindu/Buddhist festivals and is celebrated with much gusto in the Darjeeling hills. On this day, processions begin at the various Buddhist monasteries, or gumpas, and congregate at the Chowrasta (Darjeeling) Mall. The Lamas chant mantras and sound their bugles, and students, as well as people from every community, carry the holy books or pustaks on their heads. Besides Buddha Purnima, Dashain, or Dusshera, Holi, Diwali, Losar, Namsoong or the Lepcha New Year, and Losoong are the other major festivals of the Darjeeling Himalayan region.[224]

Poush Mela is a popular winter festival of Shantiniketan, with performances of folk music, Baul songs, dance, and theatre taking place throughout the town.[224]

Ganga Sagar Mela coincides with the Makar Sankranti, and hundreds of thousands of Hindu pilgrims converge where the river Ganges meets the sea to bathe en masse during this fervent festival.[223]

Education

Main articles: Education in West Bengal and Universities and colleges of West Bengal

University of Calcutta, the oldest public university of India.

The front entrance to the academic block of NUJS, Kolkata.

Prajna Bhavan, housing the School of Mathematical Sciences and School of RKMVU.

West Bengal schools are run by the state government or private organisations, including religious institutions. Instruction is mainly in English or Bengali, though Urdu is also used, especially in Central Kolkata. Secondary schools are affiliated with the Council for the Indian School Certificate Examinations (CISCE), the Central Board for Secondary Education (CBSE), the National Institute of Open School (NIOS), West Bengal Board of Secondary Education, or the West Bengal Board of Madrasah Education.[227]

As of 2016 85% of children within the 6 to 17-year age group attend school (86% do so in urban areas and 84% in rural areas). School attendance is almost universal among the 6 to 14-year age group then drops to 70% with the 15 to 17-year age group. There is a gender disparity in school attendance in the 6 to 14-year age group, more girls than boys are attending school. In Bengal, 71% of women aged 15–49 years and 81% of men aged 15–49 years are literate. Only 14% of women aged 15–49 years in West Bengal have completed 12 or more years of schooling, compared with 22% of men. 22% of women and 14% of men age 15–49 years have never attended school.[228]

St. Joseph's School, Darjeeling

Some of the notable schools in the city are: La Martiniere Calcutta, Calcutta Boys' School, St. James' School (Kolkata), St. Xavier's Collegiate School, and Loreto House, Loreto Convent, Asansol some of which rank amongst the best schools in the country.[229] Many of the schools in Kolkata and Darjeeling are colonial-era establishments housed in buildings that are exemplars of neo-classical architecture. Darjeeling's schools include: St. Paul's, St. Joseph's North Point, Goethals Memorial School, and Dow Hill in Kurseong.[230]

West Bengal has eighteen universities.[231][232] Kolkata has played a pioneering role in the development of the modern education system in India. It was the gateway to the revolution of European education during the British Raj.[233] Sir William Jones established the Asiatic Society in 1794 to promote oriental studies. People such as Ram Mohan Roy, David Hare, Ishwar Chandra Vidyasagar, Alexander Duff and William Carey played leading roles in setting up modern schools and colleges in the city.[224]

The University of Calcutta, the oldest public university in India, has 136 affiliated colleges. Fort William College was established in 1810. The Hindu College was established in 1817. The Lady Brabourne College was established in 1939. The Scottish Church College, the oldest Christian liberal arts college in South Asia, started in 1830. In 1855 the Hindu College was renamed the Presidency College.[234] The state government granted it university status in 2010 and it was renamed Presidency University. Kazi Nazrul University was established in 2012. The University of Calcutta and Jadavpur University are prestigious technical universities.[235] Visva-Bharati University at Santiniketan is a central university and an institution of national importance.[236]

The Auditorium at Indian Institute of Management Calcutta

Other higher education institutes of importance in West Bengal include: St. Xavier's College, Kolkata, Indian Institute of Foreign Trade, Indian Institute of Management Calcutta (the first IIM), Indian Institute of Science Education and Research, Kolkata, Indian Statistical Institute, Indian Institute of Technology Kharagpur (the first IIT), Indian Institute of Engineering Science and Technology, Shibpur (the first IIEST), Indian Institute of Information Technology, Kalyani, National Institute of Technology, Durgapur, National Institute of Technical Teachers' Training and Research, Kolkata, National Institute of Pharmaceutical Education and Research, Kolkata, and West Bengal National University of Juridical Sciences. In 2003 the state government supported the creation of West Bengal University of Technology, West Bengal University of Health Sciences, West Bengal State University, and Gour Banga University.[237]

Jadavpur University (Focus area—Mobile Computing and Communication and Nano-science), and the University of Calcutta (Modern Biology) are among two of the fifteen universities selected under the "University with Potential for Excellence" scheme. University of Calcutta (Focus Area—Electro-Physiological and Neuro-imaging studies including mathematical modelling) has also been selected under the "Centre with Potential for Excellence in a Particular Area" scheme.[238]

In addition, the state is home to Kalyani University, The University of Burdwan, Vidyasagar University, and North Bengal University all well as established and nationally renowned schools to cover education needs at the district level and the Indian Institute of Science Education and Research, Kolkata. Apart from this there is a Deemed university run by the Ramakrishna mission named Ramakrishna Mission Vivekananda University at Belur Math.[239]

There are several research institutes in Kolkata. The Indian Association for the Cultivation of Science is the first research institute in Asia. C. V. Raman was awarded the Nobel Prize for his discovery (Raman Effect) done at the IACS. The Bose Institute, Saha Institute of Nuclear Physics, S. N. Bose National Centre for Basic Sciences, Indian Institute of Chemical Biology, Central Glass and Ceramic Research Institute, Central Mechanical Engineering Research Institute Durgapur, Central Research Institute for Jute and Allied Fibers, National Institute of Research on Jute and Allied Fibre Technology, Central Inland Fisheries Research Institute, National Institute of Biomedical Genomics (NIBMG), Kalyani, and the Variable Energy Cyclotron Centre are the most prominent.[237]

Notable scholars who were born, worked, or studied in the geographic area of the state include physicists: Satyendra Nath Bose, Meghnad Saha,[240] and Jagadish Chandra Bose;[241] chemist Prafulla Chandra Roy;[240] statisticians Prasanta Chandra Mahalanobis and Anil Kumar Gain;[240] physician Upendranath Brahmachari;[240] educator Ashutosh Mukherjee;[242] and Nobel laureates Rabindranath Tagore,[243] C. V. Raman,[241] and Amartya Sen.[244]

Media

In 2005 West Bengal had 505 published newspapers,[245] of which 389 were in Bengali.[245] Ananda Bazar Patrika, published in Kolkata with 1,277,801 daily copies, has the largest circulation for a single-edition, regional language newspaper in India.[245] Other major Bengali newspapers are: Bartaman, Sangbad Pratidin, Aajkaal, Jago Bangla, Uttarbanga Sambad, and Ganashakti. Major English language newspapers include The Telegraph, The Times of India, Hindustan Times, The Hindu, The Statesman, The Indian Express, and Asian Age. Some prominent financial dailies such as: The Economic Times, Financial Express, Business Line, and Business Standard are widely circulated. Vernacular newspapers such as those in Hindi, Nepali, Gujarati, Odia, Urdu, and Punjabi are also read by a select readership.[246]

Doordarshan is the state-owned television broadcaster. Multi system operators provide a mix of Bengali, Nepali, Hindi, English, and international channels via cable. Bengali 24-hour television news channels include ABP Ananda, News18 Bangla, Tara Newz, Kolkata TV, News Time, Zee 24 Ghanta, Mahuaa Khobor, CTVN Plus, Channel 10, and R Plus.[247][248] All India Radio is a public radio station.[248] Private FM stations are available only in cities like Kolkata, Siliguri, and Asansol.[248] Vodafone, Airtel, BSNL, Jio, Reliance Communications, Uninor, Aircel, MTS India, Idea Cellular, and Tata DoCoMo are available cellular phone providers. Broadband Internet is available in select towns and cities and is provided by the state-run BSNL and by other private companies. Dial-up access is provided throughout the state by BSNL and other providers.[249]

Sports

Main article: Sports in West Bengal

Salt Lake Stadium / Vivekananda Yuva Bharati Krirangan, Kolkata

Cricket and association football are popular sports in the state. West Bengal, unlike most other states of India, is noted for its passion and patronage of football.[250][251][252] Kolkata is one of the major centres for football in India[253] and houses top national clubs such as Mohun Bagan Athletic Club, East Bengal Club and Mohammedan Sporting Club.[254]

West Bengal has several large stadiums. Eden Gardens was one of only two 100,000-seat cricket stadiums in the world;[255] renovations before the 2011 Cricket World Cup reduced the capacity to 66,000.[256] The stadium is the home to various cricket teams such as the Kolkata Knight Riders, the Bengal cricket team, and the East Zone. The 1987 Cricket World Cup final was hosted in Eden Gardens. The Calcutta Cricket and Football Club is the second-oldest cricket club in the world.[257]

Vivekananda Yuba Bharati Krirangan (VYBK), is a multipurpose stadium in Kolkata, with a current capacity of 85,000. It is the largest stadium in India by seating capacity.[258] Before its renovation in 2011, it was the second largest football stadium in the world, having a seating capacity of 120,000. It has hosted many national and international sporting events like the SAF Games of 1987 and the 2011 FIFA friendly football match between Argentina and Venezuela featuring Lionel Messi.[259] In 2008 legendary German goalkeeper, Oliver Kahn played his farewell match on this ground.[260] The stadium hosted the final match of the 2017 FIFA U-17 World Cup.

Notable sports persons from West Bengal include former Indian national cricket team captain Sourav Ganguly, Pankaj Roy, Olympic tennis bronze medallist Leander Paes, and chess grand master Dibyendu Barua.[250][251][252]

Panoramic View of the Eden Gardens Stadium during IPL 2008

Muzaffarpur (pronunciation (help·info)) is a city located in Muzaffarpur district in the Tirhut region of the Indian state of Bihar.[2][1] It serves as the headquarters of the Tirhut division, the Muzaffarpur district and the Muzaffarpur Railway District. It is the fourth most populous city in Bihar.

Muzaffarpur is famous for Shahi lychees and is known as the Lychee Kingdom.[4][5] Shahi litchi is set to become the fourth product from Bihar, after jardalu mango, katarni rice and Magahi paan (betel leaf) to get the Geographical Indication (GI) tag. It is situated on the banks of the perennial Burhi Gandak River, which flows from the Someshwar Hills[6] of the Himalayas.

Contents

1History

1.1Etymology

1.2After Independence

2Geography

3Climate

4Economy

4.1Lychee

5Demographics

6Transport

6.1Railways

6.2Roads

7Notable people

8See also

9References

10External links

History

Muzaffarpur's significance in Indian civilisation is due to its position between cultural and spiritual influences, and is a melting pot of Hindu and Islamic culture. Muzaffarpur has had prominent Indian political leaders, such as Rajendra Prasad, George Fernandes and J. B. Kripalani. The vernacular languages of the region are Maithili and Bajjika, as per the linguist George Grierson;[7], derived from the language of the Vedic Vrijji confederation.

Etymology

The current city was established in 1875 during the British Raj for administrative convenience, by dividing the Tirhut district and was named after an aumil, Muzaffar Khan; thus the city came to be known as Muzaffarpur.[8]

After Independence

In 1972, the Sitamarhi and Vaishali districts were split off from Muzaffarpur.[9]

Geography

Muzaffarpur is located at 26°07′N 85°24′E.[10] The city lies in a highly active seismic zone of India. In the disastrous earthquake on 15 January 1934, much of the town suffered severe damage and many lives were lost.[11] It has an average elevation of 47 meters (154 feet). This saucer shaped, low-centered town lies on the great Indo-Gangetic plains of Bihar, over Himalayan silt and sand brought by the glacier-fed and rain-fed meandering rivers of the Himalayas.

Climate

Muzaffarpur has humid subtropical climate (Cfa) under Köppen climate classification. The summer, between April and June, is extremely hot and humid (28/40 °C, 90% max.) and winter is pleasantly cool, around 06/20 °C. Rainfall in Muzaffarpur Town is comparatively less to the other parts of Bihar.

hideClimate data for Muzaffarpur

MonthJanFebMarAprMayJunJulAugSepOctNovDecYear

Record high °C (°F)29
(84)39
(102)40
(104)43
(109)48
(118)46
(115)52
(126)40
(104)39
(102)44
(111)39
(102)29
(84)52
(126)

Average high °C (°F)22
(72)26
(79)32
(90)37
(99)44
(111)40
(104)36
(97)33
(91)32
(90)32
(90)29
(84)24
(75)32
(90)

Daily mean °C (°F)18.5
(65.3)20.8
(69.4)25.0
(77.0)27.7
(81.9)27.9
(82.2)28.0
(82.4)28.4
(83.1)28.4
(83.1)28.4
(83.1)27.0
(80.6)23.4
(74.1)19.8
(67.6)25.3
(77.5)

Average low °C (°F)06
(43)12
(54)17
(63)22
(72)25
(77)27
(81)26
(79)26
(79)26
(79)22
(72)15
(59)07
(45)19
(67)

Record low °C (°F)1
(34)5
(41)10
(50)15
(59)16
(61)16
(61)22
(72)18
(64)21
(70)9
(48)8
(46)4
(39)1
(34)

Average precipitation mm (inches)12
(0.5)17
(0.7)7
(0.3)16
(0.6)42
(1.7)185
(7.3)339
(13.3)259
(10.2)242
(9.5)39
(1.5)17
(0.7)7
(0.3)1,182
(46.6)

Source: Muzaffarpur Weather

Economy

In 2006 the Ministry of Panchayati Raj named Muzaffarpur one of the country's 250 most backward districts (out of a total of 640).[12] It is one of the 36 districts in Bihar currently receiving funds from the Backward Regions Grant Fund Programme (BRGF).[12]

Lychee

Lychee garden in Muzaffarpur

The lychee crop, which is available from May to June, is mainly cultivated in the districts of Muzaffarpur and surrounding districts. Cultivation of litchi covers approximately an area of about 25,800 hectares producing about 300,000 tonnes every year. Litchi are exported to big cities of India like Bombay, Kolkata, and even to other countries. India's share in the world litchi market amounts to less than 1%. The names of the litchi produced in Muzaffarpur are Shahi and China. The fruits are known for excellent aroma and quality.[13]

Bihar's contribution in the production of lychee in about 40 percent of lychee produced in India.[14]

Bihar has emerged as a brewery hub with major domestic and foreign firms setting up production units in the state. Vijay Mallya's group, United Breweries Group, is setting up a production unit to make litchi-flavoured wine, in Muzaffarpur in 2012. The company has leased litchi gardens.[15]

Muzaffarpur based Prabhat Zarda Factory is one of the leading tobacco manufacturers of India.[16]

Demographics

As of the 2011 India census,[17] Muzaffarpur had a population of 393,724.[1] Males constituted 52.96% (208,509) of the population and females 47.04% (185,215).[1] Muzaffarpur had a literacy rate of 74.74%. Male literacy was 77.99%, and female literacy was 71.08%.[1]

Transport

Railways

Aerial view of Muzaffarpur Junction with sunset view

Muzaffarpur Junction railway station is a main railway junction, with two suburban stations, Ram Dayalu Nagar and Narayanpur Anant (Sherpur). It is well connected to major cities of Bihar like Patna, Bhagalpur, Gaya, Chakia , motihari and Darbhanga.

Roads

Road connecting New Zero Mile with NH-57

National Highway 57 (India) comes via Gorakhpur, Motihari, Chakia and crosses Muzaffarpur and National Highway 57 (India) goes to Darbhanga, Purnia. The East–West Corridor crosses Muzaffarpur thus connecting it to all the major towns and cities in India. National Highway 77 (India) starting from Hajipur passes through Muzaffarpur and connects Muzaffarpur to Sitamarhi. National Highway 28 (India) connects Muzaffarpur to Barauni, all 6 National Highways having junction there.

Notable people

Yogendra Shukla revolutionary, Indian freedom movement activist, served time at Kalapani

Basawon Singh (Sinha) revolutionary, Indian freedom movement activist

Rajendra Prasad, India's first President

Baikunth Shukla revolutionary hanged by the British in 1934

Rambriksh Benipuri Indian freedom movement activist, eminent writer of Hindi literature

Kishori Sinha Indian politician and educationalist

Maghfoor Ahmad Ajazi, political activist

Janki Ballabh Shastri, Hindi poet, writer and critic

Chandeshwar Prasad Narayan Singh, diplomat and freedom fighter

Devaki Nandan Khatri, the author of Chandrakanta (in Hindi)

Jubba Sahni, freedom fighter

Mridula Sinha, Governor of Goa (2014–present)

Veena Devi, Indian politician, Member of 17th Lok Sabha

Dinesh Prasad Singh, Indian politician

Aishwarya Nigam, a Bollywood playback singer

Shahbaz Nadeem, Indian cricketer

Sudhir Kumar Chaudhary, sports spectator and fan of the Indian Cricket Team

Shreya Narayan, Bollywood actress

Arunabh Kumar, Founder and ex-CEO of TVF

Subrat Saurabh, a writer.

Rajendra Prasad

For other uses, see Rajendra Prasad (disambiguation).

Rajendra Prasad

1st President of India

In office

26 January 1950 – 13 May 1962

Prime MinisterJawaharlal Nehru

Vice PresidentSarvepalli Radhakrishnan

Preceded byPosition established

C. Rajagopalachari as the Governor General of India

Succeeded bySarvepalli Radhakrishnan

Personal details

Born3 December 1884

Ziradei, Bengal Presidency, British India

(present-day Bihar, India)

Died28 February 1963 (aged 78)

Patna, Bihar, India

Political partyIndian National Congress

Spouse(s)

Rajavanshi Devi

(m. 1896; died 1961)

Alma materUniversity of Calcutta

AwardsBharat Ratna (1962)

Rajendra Prasad (3 December 1884 – 28 February 1963) was the first President of India, in office from 1950 to 1962.[1] He was an Indian political leader and lawyer by training. Prasad joined the Indian National Congress during the Indian Independence Movement and became a major leader from the region of Bihar. A supporter of Mahatma Gandhi, Prasad was imprisoned by British authorities during the Salt Satyagraha of 1931 and the Quit India movement of 1942. After the 1946 elections, Prasad served as Minister of Food and Agriculture in the central government. Upon independence in 1947, Prasad was elected as President of the Constituent Assembly of India, which prepared the Constitution of India and served as its provisional parliament.

When India became a republic in 1950, Prasad was elected its first president by the Constituent Assembly. Following the general election of 1951, he was elected president by the electoral college of the first Parliament of India and its state legislatures. As president, Prasad established a tradition of non-partisanship and independence for the office-bearer, and retired from Congress party politics. Although a ceremonial head of state, Prasad encouraged the development of education in India and advised the Nehru government on several occasions. In 1957, Prasad was re-elected to the presidency, becoming the only president to serve two full terms.[2]

Contents

1Early life

2Student life

3Career

3.1As a teacher

3.2As a lawyer

3.3Role in the Independence Movement

4First President of Indian Republic

5Literary contributions

6See also

7References

8Further reading

9External links

Early life[edit]

Rajendra Prasad[3] was a landholding & rich Kayastha Hindu[4] and born in Zeradai, in the Siwan district of Bihar. His father, Mahadev Sahai, was a scholar of both Sanskrit and Persian languages. His mother, Kamleshwari Devi, was a devout woman who would tell stories from the Ramayana and Mahabharata to her son. He was the youngest child and had one elder brother and three elder sisters. His mother died when he was a child and his elder sister then took care of him.[5][6]

Student life[edit]

When Prasad was five years old, his parents placed him under the tutelage of a Moulavi, an accomplished Muslim scholar, to learn the Persian language, Hindi and arithmetic. After the completion of traditional elementary education, he was sent to the Chapra District School. Meanwhile, in June 1896, at an early age of 12, he was married to Rajavanshi Devi. He, along with his elder brother, Mahendra Prasad, then went to study at T.K. Ghosh's Academy in Patna for a period of two years. He secured first in the entrance examination to the University of Calcutta and was awarded Rs. 30 per month as a scholarship.

Prasad joined the Presidency College, Calcutta in 1902, initially as a science student. He passed the F. A. under the University of Calcutta in March 1904 and then graduated with a first division from there in March 1905.[7] Impressed by his intellect, an examiner once commented on his answer sheet that the "examinee is better than examiner".[8] Later he decided to focus on the study of arts and did his M.A. in Economics with a first division from the University of Calcutta in December 1907. There he lived with his brother in the Eden Hindu Hostel. A devoted student as well as a public activist, he was an active member of The Dawn Society.[9] It was due to his sense of duty towards his family and education that he refused to join Servants of India Society, as it was during that time when his mother had died as well as his sister became a widow at the age of nineteen and had to return to her parents' home. Prasad was instrumental in the formation of the Bihari Students Conference in 1906 in the hall of the Patna College. It was the first organization of its kind in India and produced[10] important leaders from Bihar like Anugrah Narayan Sinha and Krishna Singh who played a prominent role in the Champaran Movement and Non-cooperation Movement. The organization provided political leadership to bihar in the upcoming years.

Career[edit]

As a teacher[edit]

(Sitting L to R) Prasad and Anugrah Narayan Sinha during Mahatma Gandhi's 1917 Champaran DJ Satyagraha

Rajendra Prasad served in various educational institutions as a teacher. After completing his M.A in economics, he became a professor of English at the Langat Singh College of Muzaffarpur in Bihar and went on to become the principal. However, later on he left the college to undertake legal studies and entered the Ripon College, Calcutta (now the Surendranath Law College). In 1909, while pursuing his law studies in Kolkata he also worked as Professor of Economics at Calcutta City College. In 1915, Prasad appeared in the examination of Masters in Law, passed the examination and won a gold medal. He completed his Doctorate in Law from Allahabad University in 1937.[11]

As a lawyer[edit]

In 1916, he joined the High Court of Bihar and Odisha. In 1917, he was appointed as one of the first members of the Senate and Syndicate of the Patna University. He also practiced law at Bhagalpur, the famous silk town in Bihar.

Statue of Dr. Rajendra Prasad, Calcutta High Court.

Role in the Independence Movement[edit]

This section needs additional citations for verification. Please help improve this article by adding citations to reliable sources. Unsourced material may be challenged and removed.

Find sources: "Rajendra Prasad" – news · newspapers · books · scholar · JSTOR (January 2014) (Learn how and when to remove this template message)

Jawaharlal Nehru, Bhulabhai Desai, and Rajendra Prasad (centre) at the AICC Session, April 1939

Prasad's first association with Indian National Congress was during 1906 annual session organised in Calcutta, where he participated as a volunteer, while studying in Calcutta. Formally, he joined the Indian National Congress in the year 1911, when the annual session was again held in Calcutta. During the Lucknow Session of Indian National Congress held in 1916, he met Mahatma Gandhi. During one of the fact-finding missions at Champaran, Mahatma Gandhi asked him to come with his volunteers. He was so greatly moved by the dedication, courage and conviction of Mahatma Gandhi that as soon as the motion of Non-Cooperation was passed by Indian National Congress in 1920, he retired from his lucrative career of lawyer as well as his duties in the university to aid the movement.

He also responded to the call by Gandhi to boycott Western educational establishments by asking his son, Mrityunjaya Prasad, to drop out of his studies and enrol himself in Bihar Vidyapeeth, an institution he along with his colleagues founded on the traditional Indian model.[12]

During the course of the independence movement, he interacted with Rahul Sankrityayan, a writer, and polymath. Rahul Sankrityayan was greatly influenced by Prasad's intellectual powers, finding him to be a guide and guru. In many of his articles he mentioned about his meeting with Sankrityayan and narrated about his meetings with Sankrityayan. He wrote articles for the revolutionary publications Searchlight and the Desh and collected funds for these papers. He toured widely, explaining, lecturing, and exhorting the principles of the independence movement.[citation needed]

He took an active role in helping people affected by the 1914 floods that struck Bihar and Bengal. When an earthquake affected Bihar on 15 January 1934, Prasad was in jail. During that period, he passed on the relief work to his close colleague Anugrah Narayan Sinha.[citation needed] He was released two days later and set up Bihar Central Relief Committee on 17 January 1934, and took on the task of raising funds to help the affected people. After the 31 May 1935 Quetta earthquake, when he was forbidden to leave the country due to government's order, he set up the Quetta Central Relief Committee in Sindh and Punjab under his own presidency.

He was elected as the President of the Indian National Congress during the Bombay session in October 1934. He again became the president when Netaji Subhash Chandra Bose resigned in 1939. On 8 August 1942, Congress passed the Quit India Resolution in Bombay which led to the arrest of many Indian leaders. He was arrested in Sadaqat Ashram, Patna and sent to Bankipur Central Jail. After remaining incarcerated for nearly three years, he was released on 15 June 1945.

After the formation of Interim Government of 12 nominated ministers under the leadership of Jawaharlal Nehru on 2 September 1946, he was allocated the Food and Agriculture department. He was elected by the President of Constituent Assembly on 11 December 1946.[13] On 17 November 1947 he became Congress President for a third time after J. B. Kripalani submitted his resignation.

Between 1958 and 1960, President Prasad led 5 state visits to Japan, Ceylon, USSR, Indo-China, Malaya and Indonesia.[14]

First President of Indian Republic[edit]

Two and a half years after independence, on 26 January 1950, the Constitution of independent India was ratified and Prasad was elected the nation's first president. Unfortunately, on the night of 25 January 1950, a day before the Republic Day of India, his sister Bhagwati Devi died. He arranged her cremation but only after his return from the parade ground.

As President of India, he duly acted as required by the Constitution, independent of any political party. He travelled the world extensively as an ambassador of India, building diplomatic rapport with foreign nations. He was re-elected for two consecutive terms in 1952 and 1957, and remains only President of India to achieve this feat. The Mughal Gardens at the Rashtrapati Bhavan were open to public for about a month for the first time during his tenure, and since then it has been a big attraction for people in Delhi and other parts of the country.[15]

Prasad acted independently of politics, following the expected role of the president as required the constitution. Following the tussle over the enactment of the Hindu Code Bill, he took a more active role in state affairs. In 1962, after serving twelve years as the president, he announced his decision to retire. After relinquishing the office of the President of India on May 1962, he returned to Patna on 14 May 1962 and preferred to stay in the campus of Bihar Vidyapeeth.[16] He was subsequently awarded the Bharat Ratna, the nation's highest civilian award.

He died on 28 February 1963. Rajendra Smriti Sangrahalaya in Patna is dedicated to him.[17]

Printed by Libri Plureos GmbH in Hamburg, Germany